God's Nature: Sonlight Sunlight

Christian Concepts Series

Robert Lloyd Russell

Published by LCL Company NW, 2023.

Also by Robert Lloyd Russell

Bible Character Series
Samson: Spirit-Controlled to Self-Centered
Peter: Failure to Faith

Christian Concepts Series
God's Church: Christ's Pearl
God's Nature: Sonlight Sunlight
God's Child: Like a Tree

Christian Growth Series
God's Desire: How To Please God
God's Light: How To Respond
Christ's Disciple: How To Finish Strong

Christian Theology Series
Christ's Blood: 7+ Amazing Benefits
Pride: Good and Bad
Temptation: 50+ Tips

Missions
Jim Elliot: Recorded Messages

Watch for more at www.booksrlr.com.

Table of Contents

To:

Linda and Laura

my two wonderful daughters

While every precaution has been taken in the preparation of this book, the publisher assumes no responsibility for errors or omissions, or for damages resulting from the use of the information contained herein.

GOD'S NATURE: Sonlight Sunlight

eBook: 2020-January-6, 20210102, 20230719

Print: 2023-August-01

Note: This book is an update of the first half of the printed book *GOD LIGHT: Sunlight Sonlight*. The second half has been released as an eBook entitled *SONLIGHT SUNLIGHT: Response to Light*.

Copyright © 2020 Robert Lloyd Russell

Written by Robert Lloyd Russell

Cover Photo: Public Domain

NOTES: [1] For consistency and clarity, names and pronouns of God have been capitalized throughout including in Bible versions which do not follow that practice. [2] The author capitalizes three other words: "Word" when speaking of God's Word; "Church" when speaking of the Church universal; and "Cross" when referring to the Cross of Calvary. [3] *Italicized* words and [bracketed words] in Scripture have been added by the author. [4] The author does not abbreviate the names of Bible books since abbreviations can be unknown to some readers. [5] The author chooses to use a lot of Scripture quotations based on his belief that the Word of God and the Spirit of God are the two dominant factors in changing lives and growing the lives of Christians.

We hope you enjoy this book. Robert Lloyd Russell's goal is to provide high-quality, thought-provoking books that connect truth to real life needs and challenges. For more information on his other books based on Biblical interpretation and application, please visit his author's website booksrlr.

If you find value in this book, please consider writing an online review. The author would be grateful.

> *This is the message*
> *we have heard from Him*
> *and declare to you,*
> *that **God is light** and*
> *in Him is no darkness at all.*
>
> 1 John 1:5

Reader Responses and Literary Awards

To the earlier printed version *God Light*

First there was Tozer with *The Knowledge of the Holy,* and then Packer gave us *Knowing God,* and now Russell has taken us further with *God Light.*

There is a tremendous need for a book on this subject. We have witnessed the publication of many books around the statement "God is Love," but I cannot recall ever seeing one around the statement "God is Light." It is important that these two attributes of God be brought into conjunction with each other because it is really impossible to discuss love intelligently without understanding light.

~ Dr. Earl D. Radmacher, General Editor, Nelson Study Bible/New King James Study Bible

This is truly amazing. I marvel at the wisdom God has given you and the talent to put it on paper in a meaningful/fascinating way. I have anything but a scientific mind! I found myself saying out loud, "Wow, that's amazing," many times. I worked through the technical only to be thrilled by the application at the end of each chapter. The parallel of God and His Son to the sun is brilliant! I know it's in God's Word but you have brilliantly explored His message and made it meaningful to an "un-brilliant" person such as myself!

You have opened my eyes to the light around me. Yesterday, as I looked at the clouds casting shadows on the earth, I thought of the truths you have taught me. I look at ordinary things differently. I have already used many of the truths in my mentoring and find myself sharing your thoughts in everyday conversation.

This is so rich! ... This is great! ... Wonderful! ... Mind boggling to say the least! ... Great material for discussion! ... Application pieces are truly inspired!

~ Elizabeth Hightower, Women's Ministries Leader, Laurelwood Baptist Church

He obviously is hitting on all twelve cylinders! What an exciting insight into Christ as the light of the world. Thank God for people like this who have the background to illuminate some of these Biblical concepts.

~ Dr. Joe Aldrich, President, Multnomah Bible College & Biblical Seminary

I was utterly fascinated... I am impressed with the work that you have done, with the directionality it has... I do believe that you have an important message which could be greatly used of the Spirit of God in the world today both among the Christian community and in pre-evangelism of the world.

~ Dr. Ronald Barclay Allen, Senior Professor of Bible Exposition, Dallas Seminary

It is must reading.

~ Richard C. Halverson, Chaplain, U.S. Senate

The content is terrific... This is a timely book... There is so much content that many other books and articles could be written from small parts of it.

~ Dr. Freeman L. Schmitt, Senior Pastor

I got so involved in the subject and read with such great interest that I had trouble reading it critically for accuracy.

~ Maury J. Merrick, Optics Professor & Consultant

I find it most inspirational. I can't profess to knowing anything of physics, never having studied the subject: but the explicit way in which you describe it all – I feel I am able to understand... You make the reader think, and that is a great talent.

~ Evelyn Cox, homemaker

I loved the book *God Light*!... It is very well written and very understandable. Without seeming condescending or talking down to anyone he gets the point across. The Josh McDowell book, *Evidence That Demands a Verdict,* is good too... as soon as I finish it I plan on reading *God Light* again. It's definitely the better of the two.

~ Bobby Glasgow, inmate

Awards

Gold Medal Winner, Christian Non-Fiction, *2013 Readers' Favorite* Award.

Winner, Religion—Non-Fiction, *Beverly Hills Book Award.*

Reviewers Choice Award, Religion—Eastern/Western, *2012 Reader Views Award.*

Best Book, Religion—Christianity, *2012 World Book Award.*

Runner-Up, Religion—Christianity, *2012 USA Best Book Awards.*

Finalist, Book—Biblical Studies, *2013 The Word Guild* (Canada).

Preface

Starting a new position is always a challenge—but this time I was in foreign territory. I had been named Camera Engineering Manager of a Fortune 500 firm. Although I possessed engineering management experience and was an avid amateur photographer, I knew virtually nothing about optics and the theories of light. It was a time of intense technical study.

Simultaneously I became intrigued with the Apostle John's statement in 1 John 1:5 that "God is light." What did John mean? Is there something more to this statement than meets the eye? Did the Holy Spirit of God inspire John to write three simple words that were packed with meaning beyond what John could fully understand? As I studied physical light, these questions remained prevalent in my thinking.

Virtually all Christians would agree that God is love, God is light, and God is life (1 John 4:8, 1:5, 5:12). These three concepts have been acknowledged by hymn-writers and poets for centuries. However, I found it curious that when it comes to books, literally thousands have been written on the subject God is love and on the new life that God makes available, but precious little has been penned about God is light.

In my quest I came to understand that some of the characteristics of physical light help us to understand God's nature and give new meaning to John's phrase, "God is light."

It is significant that when the apostle whom Jesus loved wrote "God is light," he gave us his purpose for writing this epistle in the previous verse, "We write this to make our joy complete." It is my desire that contemplating the nature of God as seen in the Apostle John's statement "God is Light" will bring joy to each reader.

This book may be considered a series of short essays about God light, each essay designed to provoke further thinking. The short chapters are relatively broad strokes of a brush; it is left up to you, the reader, to add details, highlights, and clarification through personal study, prayer, meditation, and life experiences. It is my prayer that such a process will allow truth to be revealed in a new and refreshing way, and in the process, "your joy might be complete."

Acknowledgements

Many individuals have influenced the direction of this book over the more than a quarter century that I have contemplated the parallels between natural light and spiritual light. (The original manuscript was completed in 1980-82.) Space permits listing only those of greatest influence.

Jim Elliot, the martyred missionary to Ecuador—was my Sunday School teacher as a young boy and a life-long example. Specifically, Jim modeled the need to take responsibility for thinking deeply about spiritual things.

Dr. Earl Radmacher has been a supportive friend and a tremendous encourager over the many years the manuscript has been developed.

Reviewers of the manuscript listed alphabetically include, Bob DeViney, Elizabeth Hightower, Warren and Betty Manley, Dr. Maurie M. Merrick, Sue Parry, and Dr. Earl D. Radmacher.

My daughters Linda and Laura have offered support, encouragement, and illustrations. Years later my then five-year-old granddaughter Abigail wrote the following poem which she entitled "God is Light:"

> God loves you and me.
> God loves everything.
> When we stumble in the darkness
> We will see that God is light.
> When I am afraid
> I will trust in God.
> Even when we disobey
> God still loves us.
> I love God.

I have been truly blessed by a family that has supported me and personally sacrificed throughout many years.

Connie, my wife, has been the single most important person of influence. Her great copy-editing skills, patience, and willingness to offer constructive criticism even when it was not readily received were all essential elements. Without Connie the manuscript would never have become a book.

My sincere thanks to the co-laborers mentioned above and to all the others for providing input, encouragement, and prayer.

Introduction

Sunlight reaches earth every day quietly providing vision, warmth, and sustenance for all life. Meanwhile lightning strikes 1,000 people in the United States each year and ignites 10,000 forest fires. Thunderstorms kill more people in the U.S. than any other natural disaster. Sunshine and gentle wind are taken for granted, but in violent forms natural elements are referred to as "acts of God."

As humans we often do not consider God during good times, but the saying from the First World War has a ring of reality, "There are no atheists in fox holes."

In this book parallels between natural light and God are examined. One might ask, "Is it valid to use nature to increase our understanding of God?" There are many ways to answer this question. First, we learn in chapter one of Romans that *general revelation,* that is nature, is enough to convince any human of the existence of the Creator. Therefore, we are without excuse if we refuse to believe in God. (In addition, *special revelation,* that is the appearing of God on earth and the written Word of God, has provided additional understanding.) Second, great teachers use stories and analogies to teach principles. The greatest teacher of all, Jesus Christ, used parables and analogies extensively, many from nature.

It is important to comment briefly regarding the scientific accuracy of this book and the parallels presented between how science currently understands physical light and what the Scriptures reveal about the God who is light. First, this manuscript has been reviewed by light and optical experts. Although concepts have been simplified for easy reading, the content is accurate according to current scientific knowledge.

Second, the author is aware that scientific understanding changes over time. Therefore, it is quite possible that there may come a time when scientists learn that light does not behave exactly as they believe it does today. Should significant changes in man's understanding of light occur, it is quite possible that some of the material in this book will become dated and perhaps some sections may be found to be inaccurate.

Third and most importantly, if such an event should occur, the reader should rest assured that while our scientific understanding of light has changed, the nature of God has not changed.

Finally, it is my prayer that if such events occur, God will at that time raise up new individuals to help readers of that era understand the mysteries surrounding the God who is light.

A key question which arises then: why take the time to understand parallels between the nature of natural light as scientists understand it and the nature of God as revealed in Scripture?

Dr. Robert John Russell (no relation to this author) has written, "As in bridge building, each community, the religious and the scientific, must find bedrock in its own world, yet each must venture out toward the other, hoping that one day the two will meet at the keystone."[1]

As a side note, it is interesting to reflect upon what Werner Heisenberg, considered the father of Quantum Physics, remarked: "The first gulp from the glass of natural sciences may make you an atheist, but at the bottom of the glass, God is waiting for you."

As we understand the marvels of physical light, our understanding of the uniqueness of God light will be greatly enhanced. We will see God in a new and intriguing way.

Sunlight / Sonlight

Sunlight is an essential part of our everyday existence.

Sonlight is an essential part of the everyday existence of the followers of the Son of God.

THINK AND GROW

1. Have you ever thought deeply about physical light?

2. Have you ever thought deeply about spiritual light?

3. Have you heard or read much about the parallels between physical and spiritual light?

Prolog

The conflict of science and religion

is one between the errors in both camps.

Truth cannot contradict itself.

Jim Elliot

We are writing these things

so that you may fully share our joy.

1 John 1:4

Heaven Light

Will it be light or dark in Heaven?" asked my then five-year-old daughter Laura. It was evening and I had just tucked her into bed. As I sat on the edge of her bed, she looked up with an inquisitive innocence that communicated to me that it was a serious question.

We had developed a little game at bedtime; I would ask Laura a question regarding the Bible, and she would provide the answer. It was, I thought, a good way to communicate some Christian truths in a natural way. One of the questions that she never missed was, "What three things that characterize God's nature start with L?" Her response was always immediate, sure, and consistent, "God is love, God is light, and God is life." Because I was sure that she knew these concepts well, it bothered me to have her now pose this question, which to me had such an obvious answer.

Calmly and methodically I began to help Laura discover the answer for herself. "Well, Honey," I began, "what three things characterize the nature of God?" "But Dad," she replied, "you know I know that! What I want to know is will it be light or dark in Heaven?" "Well, Laura, what do you think?" "Dad!" her exasperated soft voice replied. As much as I didn't want to give in and spoon-feed her the answer, I replied, "Honey, since God IS light, don't you suppose it will be very, very light in heaven?"

Laura appeared to be deep in thought for a few seconds and then came her reply, "I thought it would be very, very, dark so that we would be able to see Him better!" I must admit I like her concept better than my own, and to this day when reflecting back on that moment I feel a lump in my throat.

Throughout the Bible we find man pictured as being in darkness—actually more literally "as darkness"—or spiritually blind. Those who have discovered and acted upon the truth of Jesus Christ as the Son of God are pictured oppositely as in the light—literally "as light"—with spiritual sight.

As we begin our study of parallels between sunlight and Sonlight, consider the apparent paradox: it is physically harmful to look directly at the sun, but spiritually necessary to look to the Son for direction and salvation (Numbers 21:8, John 3:14).

As a flower moves itself to face the sun, we should keep our focus on the Son. A.W. Tozer put it this way, "God made us to be like planets. Around and around they go, held together by the magnetic attraction of the sun."

May you always keep the Son in your eyes!

Sunlight / Sonlight

Sunlight dispels physical darkness.

Sonlight dispels spiritual darkness.

THINK AND GROW

What do you think? Will it be light or dark in heaven?

SONLIGHT—SUNLIGHT ATTRIBUTES

~ The Character of God ~

To the Christian nothing is commonplace;

everything is somehow miraculous.

Jim Elliot

This is the message we heard from Jesus

and now declare to you:

God is light,

and there is no darkness in Him at all.

1 John 1:5

COMMON
Yet
UNKNOWN!

1

Outside the Box

The forces of nature seem schizophrenic. Consider basic elements such as water, wind, fire, and light. Water is essential to life but can be destructive in uncontrolled flooding. Wind, which as a gentle breeze produces lovely crystal-clear smog less days, can become vicious in the form of a hurricane or typhoon. The same fire that is essential for warmth can be a merciless killer. Light, which allows us to see the beauty of interaction of the natural elements, can cause skin cancer with over exposure to its life-giving rays.

Normally gentle, light can be awesome in its power. Light is usually continuous and uniform but sometimes arrives in great instantaneous brilliant bursts of power. Generally operating in a totally silent mode, light occasionally produces great thunderous outbursts.

So begins our study of the subject of light! In the pages that follow, you find an integration of what scientists know about natural light and how theologians understand the God of the Bible. This integration results in many fascinating parallels that provide insights into both physical and spiritual light.

Some remarkable truths about natural light will be outlined. Unless you have a solid knowledge of physics, some of the characteristics of light will seem unbelievable. However, all statements about light and its attributes are accurate based upon modern scientific understanding.

Since this book is not intended as a technical textbook, concepts have been translated into everyday language. It follows therefore that we will not deal with technical detail. Rather, we will consider the overall aspects of light and its behavior from a conceptual point of view.

If you find yourself troubled by some aspects of natural light, I simply ask you to remember that the statements regarding various aspects of light are true. If some of what is presented is hard to understand from our human perspective, then please remind yourself that it is an additional parallel between natural light and spiritual light. God light, whether physical light or spiritual light, is hard to understand from a purely human point of view. To comprehend light, we must think outside the box to which we are so accustomed.

I have worked hard to present an adequate explanation of the relevant technical and theological information that the integration of the two great themes of physical and spiritual light demands. In order to present the material in as straightforward a manner as possible, you will notice an absence of charts and graphs. Mathematical formulas, diagrams, and tables have been left out with the exception of reference to Dr. Albert Einstein's famous little formula $E = mc^2$. As will be seen, this simple-appearing formula has many profound implications.

Einstein wrote, "The object of all science, whether natural science or psychology, is to coordinate our experiences and to bring them into a logical system." And I believe it is equally valid to remark that the object of all philosophy, whether rooted in religion or ethics, is to coordinate our meaning and purpose and bring them into a logical system. Such a system, in the case of religion, is referred to as theology.

God is mysterious from the human perspective—however, with an appropriate understanding, a systematic theology, the mystery of God is significantly reduced.

Sunlight / Sonlight

Sunlight enables physical vision which assists us in understanding our surroundings through the creation of a logical system of theories and beliefs about our physical environment.

Sonlight enables spiritual vision which assists us in understanding our existence through doctrines and beliefs about our spiritual environment.

THINK AND GROW

1. Do you think it is *important* for mankind to develop a set of principles or theories about our physical environment—what we call science? Why, or why not?

2. Do you think it is *possible* there is a set of principles and theories about spirituality and God, like we have for science?

3. Do you think it is *important* for mankind to understand that God—His character, nature, and revelation—can be discerned trough an intellectually honest and rigorous examination of the natural world?

4. Is there value, for the Christian and the skeptic, in considering the claims of Romans 1:19-20?

2

Explaining Light

One afternoon while seated at my computer I suddenly saw a flash of light. It seemed to have come from over my left shoulder, as if someone had taken a flash picture behind me. Without thinking much about it, I continued working until a second and third flash occurred.

I got up and looked around the house. Not seeing anything out of the ordinary, I returned to my work.

A little while later I couldn't seem to remove what seemed to be a hair hanging in front of my left eye—I even went into the bathroom and looked in the mirror to try to find it.

As the day progressed my vision became worse, blurred by "floaters" moving around in my left eye.

What was it that had flashed in my eye? Was it a physical object? I had seen the flash, but I hadn't discovered the source.

The next day my ophthalmologist explained that I had posterior vitreous detachment as well as vitreous hemorrhaging. I left his office with a brochure about "floaters and flashes."

What exactly is light? We can see it, but we can't put our hands on it or feel it.

Early in man's history, it was believed that at the end of every day, the sun died. Some time later, it was thought light was a substance in the air that precipitated out in the afternoon, thus providing night.

Another theory was that light was sent out by the eye to provide vision. A modified version of that concept was that light was a sort of radar that the eye sent out; when it struck an object, it returned to the eye.

Six centuries before Christ, the Greek philosopher, religious reformer, and mathematician Pythagoras suggested that objects somehow gave off small particles that resembled their source. He didn't explain how this occurred but reasoned that as these particles reached the eye, they somehow produced sight.

About a century later Greek philosopher and statesman Empedocles expressed his theory that sight originated at the eye, and the eye gave off something that when striking objects in its path, provided vision.

About 90 A.D., long before there were demonstrably satisfactory theories about light, the Apostle John wrote, "God is light."

During the time when Jesus walked on earth, it was believed that light was a fire-like substance that permeated the air. Light was not considered to be something passing through the air, but rather a part of the daytime atmosphere. It was believed that through some sort of mysterious action, light left the air during the night hours.

While mankind does not yet fully understand light, significant strides have been made, particularly within the last century, regarding our knowledge about light and the application of this knowledge. A substantial portion of man's total scientific knowledge has been an outgrowth of attempts to understand light. Virtually all the knowledge of our universe has been gained through the study and analysis of the light that reaches us.

Even more fundamentally, it can be said that the majority of our knowledge has been gained because of sight, which is of course only possible because of light.

Likewise, the vast majority of man's search for spiritual meaning and identity has come from his belief in God. Like the study of light, the fallout has been tremendous. This search for meaning and belief in God has directly resulted in many of the good and noble acts of men throughout the centuries.

Christians believe spiritual light is far more permanent and more substantial than physical light. The Bible calls Jesus the "Morning Star" (2 Peter 1:19; Revelation 22:16) and calls Him the "Sun of Righteousness" (Malachi 4:2). We find the face of Jesus described as "shining like the sun in full strength" (Revelation 1:16).

In the pages to follow we will see that the simple statement—God is Light—penned by the "apostle whom Jesus loved" through the prompting of the Holy Spirit, is a most meaningful statement in view of man's current knowledge. Understanding sunlight enables us to more fully understand Sonlight.

Sunlight / Sonlight

From the beginning man has sought to comprehend his physical environment. Physical light is critical to life on earth and to all scientific understanding. Today we know so much more than in the past. Scientific knowledge is growing at exponential rates. Even with all the modern advances there are many unanswered questions. For example, consider all the unanswered questions about the human body, disease, and how to cure diseases, extend life, and so forth.

From the beginning man has also asked basic questions. Why am I here? Is there more to life than meets the eye? What happens when I die? Is there more after death? The new life found in the Son of God is the critical ingredient in understanding our existence and the existence of this vast universe.

THINK AND GROW

1. Do you think John understood the implications of his declaration when the Spirit of God inspired him to write "God is light?"

2. How does John's statement "God is light" have implication regarding the inspiration of Scripture?

3. Does the Apostle John's statement "God is light" stimulate you to reconsider other passages of Scripture in a new light? Have you already used a concordance to search for those passages?

3

The Mystery of Light: Dualistic

My immediate family was understanding of my quest to understand John's statement that God is light. Daughters Linda and Laura not only accepted the hours of "Daddy locked in his library" but saw it as a personal challenge and family project. Typical is the note I found on my desk one day from then nine-year-old Linda.

To Dad,

Something I found in my test book about light might help you! (in your book)

"For thousands of years people have puzzled over the nature of light. Today one of the most widely accepted theories of light is the quantum theory, which was developed in the 20th century. The quantum theory was the brainchild of Max Planck. The essence of the theory is that when atoms are heated electrons jump back toward the center of the atom, energy in the form of light is released. This light energy is measured in units called photons or quanta."

From: Linda

Linda had come upon one of the newer theories about the nature of light.

Over the centuries the nature of light has been debated, sometimes heatedly. Eventually two theories became most prevalent. The predominant theory until about the middle of the seventeenth century was that light consisted of particles that passed through space in a straight line. English scientist Isaac Newton was one of the strongest supporters of this particle or corpuscle theory.

In 1670 Christian Huygens, a Dutch astronomer, mathematician, and physicist, produced substantial evidence for a wave theory of light. His work became foundational for our present understanding of light.

During the early nineteenth century Thomas Young, an Englishman, championed the theory that light was made up of waves. Although he had experimental evidence to support his idea, he was ridiculed, largely because his findings contradicted the revered Newton. Other scientists such as Fresnel and Foucault eventually produced evidence that tended to further support this wave theory.

In the late nineteenth century Scottish scientist James C. Maxwell developed the electromagnetic theory of light. This theory has had profound consequences throughout the entire scientific world.

By the end of the nineteenth century some scientists believed that they had discovered all the fundamental laws of nature. There is a commonly told story about the great German physicist Max Planck. As he entered the university, the head of the physics department is reported to have told him that it was hardly worth entering the field of physics anymore. The professor's reasoning was that all the important discoveries had already been made. But in 1900 Max Planck announced his *quantum theory*, which would revolutionize the world of physics. It demonstrated that light behaved like both particles and waves.

Einstein followed Planck with significant discoveries that were to impact our understanding of light. Light, it seemed, was not really made of waves, nor was it really made of particles alone; rather, somehow light was both waves and particles at the same time. This was such a paradox that even Einstein didn't entirely buy into it. Although this seemed contradictory, this dual concept began to gain acceptance, since scientific evidence would not allow the ruling out of either the wave nature or the particle nature. Today, the dual nature of light is the basis of quantum theory, a pillar of modern physics.

Scientists now accept the fact that light is *dualistic* in nature. To understand some aspects of light's behavior, the *particle theory* is necessary. This has been modified by the quantum theory to be small individual packets of energy. However, other aspects of light can only be satisfied by the *wave theory*. This has been expanded significantly in modern times, and light is now known to be a part of the electromagnetic spectrum.

British physicist Sir William Bragg is reported to have remarked that there seemed to be no recourse but to believe in waves on Monday, Wednesday, and Friday, and to use the particle theory on Tuesday, Thursday, and Saturday. Before long some anonymous wit had added, "And on Sunday we pray for enlightenment."[2] This explanation of light as being dualistic in nature continues today. "Light seems sometimes to behave like particles and other times to act like waves. Today, we think of light as having some of both properties."[3]

Out of Planck's and Einstein's work has come the idea of small packets of energy, now called photons, which is the basis for the quantum theory and much of modern-day scientific understanding. The revolution in science that continues today, including electronics and nuclear energy, is a result of their work.

Today, whether a physicist uses the wave model, or the particle model is largely a matter of convenience. The concept of "wave-particle duality" is firmly established by experimental evidence and the models of quantum mechanics.

Sunlight / Sonlight

Sunlight is both particles and waves—two very contradictory concepts.

According to the Bible the Son of God is fully God and while on earth He was fully man—two very contradictory natures.

THINK AND GROW

1. Can you think of historical examples where science has misunderstood the natural world because of their limited understanding—only later to revise their concepts?

2. Should those examples discredit the credibility of science?

3. Can you think of historical examples where people have misunderstood the Word of God because of their limited understanding?

4. Should those examples discredit the credibility of the Word of God?

4

Relativity Explains Light

The great German-born physicist Einstein was not known for faith in God or spirituality but for his remarkable insight into the physical world. Although most people know about Einstein's work in the area of physics, few are aware that he had a strong respect for the Creator. He wrote, "I do see the design of the universe as essentially a religious question, that is, one should have some kind of respect and awe for the whole business. It is very magnificent and shouldn't be taken for granted."

There is cause to believe that the reason Einstein (1879-1955) rejected *organized* religion was that he felt God was not accredited the majesty and awe that He was due. The religions of his day typically did not give proper respect to the Author of Life and Creator of the Universe.

Einstein revolutionized our understanding of gravity, time, motion, space, and the universe. Much of mankind's present knowledge about light, its speed, its importance in the overall design of our universe, and the phenomena which occur as an object approaches the speed of light, is a result of the work of Einstein. He laid the groundwork that has enabled much of the great technological advances of this century.

As a side note, it is interesting to read the words of another great scientist, Isaac Newton: "Gravity explains the motions of the planets, but it cannot explain Who set the planets in motion. God governs all things and knows all that is or can be done."

Einstein's two most important accomplishments were his theory of special relativity in 1905, which dealt with objects moving at high speed, and his theory of general relativity in 1915, dealing with gravity.

Scientific investigations since have proved that we do indeed live in a universe very similar to that which Einstein described.

Einstein's famous formula, $E = mc^2$, from his theory of special relativity, is deceptively simple in its appearance. "E" stands for "energy," "m" for "mass" (if you are not familiar with mass, think of it as weight), and "c" for the "speed of light." Light is very important in this equation; both energy and mass are variables, but light is an unchanging fundamental constant value. The speed of light is a fundamental law of nature and is as basic as gravity.

Although this little formula is simple in appearance, the consequences of its mathematical relationship are awesome in implication. Largely because of this equation, we now have a much better understanding of our sun, upon which all of life on earth is dependent. Scientists realize that virtually all of creation is literally linked to $E = mc^2$. This equation is the basis for the understanding that has produced the nuclear age with its nuclear bombs, nuclear power plants, and all of the related potential for both good and evil.

There are common misconceptions about the "theory of relativity." Two misconceptions come from its name. First, many people are accustomed to equating the word *theory* with unproven or even unfactual information. In the scientific community the word *hypothesis* is used to describe an unproven concept, and a *theory* on the contrary is well established. In fact, Einstein's theory of relativity is one of the most completely established theories in physics.

Secondly, the word *relativity* implies to many the opposite of *absolute*. "Einstein is often said to have held 'all things are relative.' He did not. 'Relativity' is in fact a thoroughly bad name for the theory. Einstein considered calling it the opposite: 'invariance theory.' He discovered what was absolute and reliable despite the apparent confusions, illusions, and contradictions produced by relative motions or action of gravity. The chief merit of the name 'relativity' is in reminding us that a scientist is unavoidably a participant in the system he is studying. Einstein gave 'the observer' his proper status in modern science."[4]

Einstein's theory of relativity, rather than claiming that things are relative, defines some absolutes. The speed of light is an absolute. This is not to imply that the speed of light does not change—it does. In saying that light travels at 286,282 miles per second, we are referring to the speed of light in a vacuum. As light travels through matter, such as glass, it slows down a very minute amount. But the speed of light is absolute. Light will always travel at the same speed in a vacuum, and it will always travel at the same speed in a specific type of glass.

The theory of relativity not only established that the speed of light is absolute or unchanging, but also established many other physical laws. The theory established and confirmed that the laws of physics are absolute in the sense that they are consistent throughout the whole universe. Einstein's theory displayed the remarkable uniformity of the universe as a whole.

"The laws of nature are the same for everyone... Astronomers can make sense of the universe and its contents only because atoms evidently behaved in *exactly* the same way billions of years ago."[5]

Our universe could not provide reliable conditions for life without an extreme amount of orderliness and consistency. This is what the theory of relativity helped to verify.

Sunlight / Sonlight

When it comes to the physical aspect of humankind, the scientific word theory is often misunderstood and inappropriately discarded. Theories have stood the test of time and have much supporting empirical evidence.

When it comes to the spiritual aspect of humankind, the religious word faith is often misunderstood and inappropriately discarded. Faith has stood the test of time and has much supporting empirical evidence.

THINK AND GROW

1. Have you ever heard comments such as, "Even Einstein believed that everything was relative?" If so, how would you now respond to such a statement?

2. How do you suppose those who say there are "no absolutes" would explain the natural laws discussed in this chapter? Would they acknowledge the self-contradiction of their statement (i.e., there are absolutely no absolutes)?

3. List five ways humans frequently exercise faith in their daily lives (example: crossing a man-made bridge built by the lowest bidder without having the knowledge of structural engineering which is necessary for a rational confidence).

5

Sunlight

One summer evening as I sat in my study, a slight movement caught my eye outside the window directly in front of me. A beautiful doe had wandered into the grassy area in our back yard, followed closely by a tiny fawn.

The fawn was playful—jumping, darting about, chasing first the wind, then moths, and even his mother—completely oblivious to the possible danger all around.

But the doe was another story: alert, constantly watching for anything that might harm her offspring. Her watchfulness and protection, unnoticed and unappreciated by the fawn, were essential to her fawn's survival.

Of all the benefits we receive from our Creator, few are as essential or remarkable as physical light, yet few are so little appreciated.

The human body is astounding in its ability and flexibility with regard to natural light. With our eyes we can distinguish tens of thousands of graduations of color, see particles of dust only one five-thousandth of an inch across, and see light reflected from paper illuminated by a single candle 1,000 feet away.

The eye is capable of adjusting focus to examine objects many miles away as easily as it can read the printed words on a page only inches away. With normal sight a person can read a book in the noontime sun on a bright day or in the quiet of the night by the light of a full moon. Yet the difference in illumination represented by these two situations is about a million to one.

Only in recent history has mankind unraveled some of the secrets of natural physical light. We have been able to make light do useful things. First came magnifiers, then lens combinations, and more recently lasers, which so control the form of energy we call light that they can cut diamonds.

The wide-spread availability of powerful computers has created new precision and efficiencies in areas such as optical lens design. Optical computer memory has become common. In the world today pulses of light transmitted through fiber optics have caused a revolution in communication systems.

Light has always been a part of our daily lives in its natural form, but now it is becoming increasingly significant regarding the various ways we have learned to make use of our knowledge of its behavior.

However, mankind still does not have full understanding of light. The more we have learned about it, the more wonderful and mysterious it has become.

The secrets of our universe all seem to be intimately connected with light. It is light's revealing power that has allowed mankind to make great scientific discoveries. All things are connected to light in mysterious and complex ways. Chemistry and electricity are intricately related to light. One thing which Einstein's formula, $E = mc^2$, clearly shows to scientists is that all matter and energy are related to light. Light is the secret to all of nature and all of life. In a remarkable way light unlocks the truth about all things.

Sunlight / Sonlight

Sunlight is a key to man's ability to observing and understanding his physical environment.

Sonlight is the key to man's ability to understand the mystery of our existence.

THINK AND GROW

1. What other objects or phenomena are generally not fully appreciated?

2. Why do you think this is the case?

3. If mankind's practical application of spiritual light from God had kept pace with our progress in applying the principles of physical light, how might our world be different? Can you think of examples in our social, political, and international affairs?

6

Sonlight

The concert hall was buzzing with the hushed voices of thousands of people anxious to hear the evening's performance by the Oregon Symphony Orchestra. My wife and I looked forward to another extraordinary concert. We were not to be disappointed.

One piece was especially good. I remember hearing early in the introduction an interesting and unique tune which was further developed throughout the piece as it was played on various instruments. Then at the end the theme came into play again, bringing a lovely conclusion to this masterful piece.

In a similar fashion woven throughout the Bible, from the very beginning to the very end, we find the concept of light in various manifestations.

It is the first thing we read about in the creation story. "Let there be light" (Genesis 1:3).

Then at the end, in the very last chapter of the Bible, we find that in heaven God Himself will be the only source of light. "There shall be no night there: They need no lamp nor light of the sun, for the Lord God gives them light" (Revelation 22:5).

Just as there are various meanings for the word today, "light" is used many ways in Scripture. One consistent use of the word is in reference to God. For instance, in the Old Testament we are told, "The Lord is my light and my salvation" (Psalm 27:1); "the light of Your countenance" (Psalm 44:3); and the prophet Isaiah wrote, "a light has shined. You have multiplied the nation and increased its joy" (Isaiah 9:2-3). "The Lord will be a light to me" (Micah 7:8); "His brightness was like the light; He had rays flashing from His hand, and there His power was hidden" (Habakkuk 3:4). Also, the Shekinah glory of God in the Holy of Holies was a supernatural light that appeared on the mercy seat, or atonement cover (Exodus 40:35).

Consider how often light is involved when God reveals Himself to man. God revealed Himself to Moses through the light of a burning bush (Exodus 3:1-4). In this instance God used the relatively dim light of fire in the form of a burning bush to reveal His brilliance to Moses because the extreme brightness of God who is light is far too intense for man to look upon. Later we read, "Now it was so, when Moses came down from Mount Sinai (and the two tablets of the Testimony were in Moses' hand when he came down from the mountain), that Moses did not know that the skin of his face shone while he talked with Him. So, when Aaron and all the children of Israel saw Moses, behold, the skin of his face shone, and they were afraid to come near him" (Exodus 34:29-30, see also 2 Corinthians 3:7-8). Even having seen only the *back* of God (Exodus 33:23), Moses was so radiant that others could not look at him!

God used the light of fire to proclaim His presence on many occasions. A pillar of fire was used to guide the nation of Israel at night (Exodus 13:21-22). On Mount Sinai God descended upon the children of Israel with fire (Exodus 19:18). God sent fire to consume Elijah's offering on Mt. Carmel (1 Kings 18:38-39). Ezekiel was given a vision of fire to warn of coming judgment (Ezekiel 1:27). And God used fire at the coming of the Holy Spirit (Acts 2:1-3). God often used the light of fire as a visual manifestation of His presence.

Another example of God revealing Himself in the form of light is seen in the New Testament account of Saul's conversion, where God's appearance was in the form of a bright light, resulting in the temporary blindness of Paul (Acts 9:3-9).

Additional examples of God as light in Scripture include: "You are resplendent with light" (Psalm 76:4 niv). "Who cover Yourself with light as with a garment" (Psalm 104:2). "They looked to Him and were radiant" (Psalm 34:5). "He will endure as long as the sun, as long as the moon, through all generations ... May His name endure forever; may it continue as long as the sun" (Psalm 72:5, 17 niv).

In the sixth chapter of Isaiah we read of the seraphim, a special type of angel. They are in the presence of God, extolling His holiness. The glory of God is so bright that Isaiah says the seraphim cover their faces with two of their six wings. Like man, the seraphim are created beings, and therefore the brightness of His glory is too much for them to observe.

This is not an exhaustive list of the Scriptures that show a relationship between God and light.

In heaven we will dwell with God, who is light, and we will then fully understand all the intricacies of both physical and spiritual light.

Sunlight / Sonlight

Sunlight is woven throughout our physical existence. Without physical light there would be no life on earth.

Sonlight is woven throughout the written Word of God. Without an understanding of the God who is light and acceptance of His Word and His work on our behalf, there is no spiritual life.

Quotes

"What is the best weather forecast? God reigns and the Son shines."

"Physically blind cannot see the sun, the spiritually blind cannot see the Son." —John MacArthur

THINK AND GROW

1. When you read the words, "God is light," what is the first attribute of God you think of?

2. What attributes of physical light can you identify that are fitting pictures of God?

3. The Bible has much to say about the Shekinah glory of God. For example, look up Exodus 40:35, Leviticus 16:2, 1 Kings 8:10, 2 Chronicles 5:13, Psalm 80:1, Isaiah 37:16, and Ezekiel 9:3. What do these verses tell you about God light and John's statement that "God is light"?

4. Look up Exodus 13:21-22 and Acts 9:3, 8-9, 18, 27; 22:6, 11; and 26:13. What relevance do these verses have with respect to Sonlight?

ATTRIBUTES
Of
LIGHT

7

Everywhere at Once: Omnipresent

Snails can move at about six inches per hour. Busy little ants scurry about at a much faster pace, and an average person walks at about three miles per hour. The fastest snakes will cover about 10 miles in an hour. A top athlete might run a mile in four minutes—15 miles per hour for a short period.

In the middle of the nineteenth century it took a covered wagon about five and one-half months to cross the United States. Later stagecoaches were able to make the same trip in just two months.

By 1870 trains could make the cross-country trip in just eleven days. In 1923 early aviators could make the trip by air in about 26 hours. In the mid-1970s the Boeing 747 was regularly making the trip in five hours. And in 1981 the space shuttle Columbia crossed above the U.S. in just eight minutes.

The 186,282 miles which light travels in one second is roughly equivalent to seven complete trips around the earth.

In our day we tend to lose the significance of large numbers. Consider the following table—each number is expressed in miles per second:

Top athlete running: 0.0042
Cheetah: 0.019
Falcon in a dive: 0.049
Speed of sound: 0.21
Speed of the moon: 0.63
Speed of light: 186,282.

At 186,282 miles per second, light travels over eleven million miles in a minute, or nearly six million million miles in a year's time. All other speeds, even the speed of sound—which is only about two-tenths of a mile in a second—are insignificant when compared to the speed of light.

Light is the fastest thing known to man. Light is so fast it appears to be instantaneous, and indeed even scientists believed light was instantaneous until the early twentieth century. Light is unusual not only in its great speed, but in its infinite acceleration. When we turn on an electric light, the light does not begin to slowly emanate from the bulb, gradually picking up speed. Rather, light is immediately traveling at 186,282 miles per second.

If we want to understand light, we must think outside our box of time, space, and matter. Light does not behave in ways to which we are accustomed, as illustrated by its extreme speed and instantaneous acceleration. Light is everywhere at once.

Modern man has grown so accustomed to these highly unusual characteristics of light that we rarely stop to contemplate or marvel at their uniqueness. We are so conditioned to the presence of light that we do not consider its unique characteristics.

When we contemplate characteristics of God's nature, we find that they are uniquely different than our human nature.

The Bible tells us that we are created in the image of God (Genesis 1:27). But He is orders of magnitude beyond us in His characteristics whether we consider aspects of intellect, emotion, or will. A newborn has been created in the image of the parents but lacks the depth of wisdom, love, and virtually all characteristics.

God behaves in ways to which we are not accustomed. "For My thoughts are not your thoughts, nor are your ways My ways,' says the

Lord. 'For as the heavens are higher than the earth, so are My ways higher than your ways, and My thoughts than your thoughts'" (Isaiah 55:8-9). "'Can anyone hide himself in secret places, so I shall not see him?' says the Lord; 'do I not fill heaven and earth?' says the Lord" (Jeremiah 23:24).

The Word of God clearly tells us that God is present everywhere, or omnipresent. It is difficult for our human minds to grasp the concept of a God who is everywhere at once. But light, with its extreme speed and instantaneous acceleration, is a most fitting symbol for a God who is everywhere without boundary.

Sunlight / Sonlight

The sun appears each morning and disappears below the horizon each evening. Sunlight allows us to see and move about in our surroundings. All energy on earth is ultimately derived from the sun.

The light of the Son; the Son of God Himself, is simultaneously everywhere present.

THINK AND GROW

1. What are the practical implications to daily living of a God who is everywhere at once?

2. In what ways does contemplation of God require you to think outside your natural constraints of time, space, and matter?

3. Look up Psalm 139:7, Jeremiah 23:24, Acts 17:24-27. What do these verses tell you about God? What are the implications of these verses?

8

The Key to All Energy: Omnipotent

Where does power come from? Energy! Then where does energy come from? All energy comes from light! Light is the key to all energy.

It is very important to understand that light does not contain energy, it *is* energy. Einstein's formula, $E = mc_2$, defines energy as the mass of an object, multiplied by the speed of light multiplied by itself. The mass of any ordinary object is quite insignificant when compared to the number resulting from multiplying the speed of light (186,282 miles per second) times the speed of light or 34,700,983,524. This simple-appearing formula $E = mc_2$ tells scientists; that light is the key to all energy.

Contrary to popular belief, the earth does not have a shortage of energy—only a shortage of readily useable energy. Consider the tremendous power in nature such as Mt. Saint Helens, the volcano which in 1980 released a small portion of its energy. In that violent 400-megaton explosion, six-tenths of a cubic mile was blown off the top of the mountain. The blast was about eight times more powerful than the largest nuclear device ever exploded. Winds from the blast, in excess of 200 miles per hour, felled enough trees to build 200,000 homes.

Geologists say that Mt. Saint Helens has erupted over twenty times during the last 4,500 years. All that released energy had its origin in the sun. All the abundant energy on the planet we call earth has come from the sun in the form of light. Energy in various forms is all around us, waiting to be apprehended and converted into useful sources.

According to the theory of relativity, no physical object could ever travel at the speed of light. A primary reason for this is that an object increases in mass as it approaches the speed of light. Because of this increase in mass, it would require an infinite amount of energy to cause any physical object to travel at the speed of light. Or in very simple terms, all the energy in the world would not be enough to propel a speck of dust at the speed of light. This is a difficult concept to comprehend, but it would be hard to find a scientist or physicist who does not accept this aspect of relativity.

Since the increase in mass as an object approaches the speed of light (and the resulting required energy) is not linear, it is not easily observed until the object is traveling at extremely high rates of speed. The closer the speed comes to the speed of light, the greater the rate of increase in energy required to travel just a tiny bit faster.

To calculate this effect, physicists use the *gamma factor*. Using the gamma factor, we can calculate the mass of an object as it approaches the speed of light. Assume for a moment that we are about to travel on a spaceship that has a mass of 200 tons as we sit upon our launch pad.

In the table below the left column is speed as a percent of the speed of light. The right column is the mass of the same spaceship in tons. As we approach the speed of light, the mass of our spaceship will increase as shown in the following table:

0%	00,200
10%	00,201
20%	00,204
30%	00,210
40%	00,218
50%	00,231
60%	00,250
70%	00,280
80%	00,333
90%	00,459
95%	00,640
99%	01,418
99.9%	04,472
99.999%	44,721
100%	Infinite

As you see, the increase in mass is most pronounced as the object attains a speed close to the speed of light. This increase in mass requires vast amounts of energy to propel until, at 100 percent of the speed of light, the infinite mass requires infinite energy! If these concepts are difficult to believe, just remember that they are accepted by physicists today.

Since light travels uniformly and ceaselessly at a fantastic speed for billions of years and never requires refueling, it provides a portrait of the all-powerful, "omnipotent," God. In order to comprehend such as a powerful being, we must be willing to think differently about time, space, and matter.

Power is a term that denotes the ability to do work. God is the all-powerful One. He has the capacity to do all that we desire. "Able to do exceedingly abundantly above all that we ask or think" (Ephesians 3:20).

God is waiting to be recognized as the one true God, powerful enough to handle all the problems of living that we face. "For since the creation of the world His invisible attributes are clearly seen, being understood by the things that are made, even His eternal power and Godhead, so that they are without excuse" (Romans 1:20).

The Apostle John told us that God is light. God is all-powerful, the Omnipotent One, the key to all energy!

~ *Quote* ~ "The same God who guides the stars in their courses, who directs the earth in orbit, who feeds the burning furnace of the sun, and keeps the stars perpetually burning with their fires – the same God has promised to supply thy strength." —unknown

Sunlight / Sonlight

Sunlight travels at such a speed that it would take an infinite amount of energy to move a tiny object a tiny distance at that speed.

Sonlight, the Son of God, is omnipotent, the all-powerful One.

THINK AND GROW

1. Are you experiencing the power of God in your life?

2. If not, what might be some of the reasons? What can you do about it?

3. Look up John 1:3; 8:12, 58; 17:5; and Colossians 1:16-17. Do these verses support the idea of an omnipotent God? Why or why not?

4. Look up Daniel 4:17, 25, 32; Psalm 33:6-9; Matthew 28:18 kjv; and Romans 1:20. Which of these verses do you find to be the most meaningful to you?

5. Is omnipotence a significant attribute of God? Why or why not?

9

Seeing Is Knowing: Omniscient

Consider the role of photosynthesis in plant life. Scientists have been able to see, literally and figuratively, how this life-giving and life-sustaining process works. It is a complex process that is going on all around us and is only possible because of light. A common everyday occurrence, photosynthesis is the source of all our food, our very basis for physical life. Without light the food that sustains us could not grow.

Photosynthesis is going on continuously inside the cells of all green plants. Each cell in the plant contains living protoplasm. The protoplasm contains numerous bodies known as chloroplasts, which are very small, less than one twenty-five-hundredth of an inch in diameter. There are over two hundred fifty million of these per square inch of a leaf.

"Assuming that on a well-grown mature elm there are 7,000,000 leaves and determining by experiment that the average area of an elm leaf is 3.25 square inches, we arrive at the astonishing figure of 22,834,000 square inches as the total leaf area of such a tree. ... The total chloroplast area in an elm tree with 7,000,000 leaves is 456,680,000 square yards, or 94,355 acres or 147.4 square miles or greater than the area of the smallest state in the Union, Rhode Island."[6]

Some of these leaves and plants are eaten by animals, transmitting energy to them for their survival. Man, in turn eats animals or plants directly and thereby obtains needed energy. The energy we call light is transmitted to plants, then to animals and humans, and eventually to the earth itself. Sunlight is the source of all the energy involved in life.

In 1897 Samuel P. Langley stated, "It is now well understood that … every manifestation of life from that of the lowest vegetable form up through animal existence, to that of man, including all his works and industries, comes from the sun."[7]

Man's knowledge about the process of photosynthesis has been gained because of his ability to see and observe the process going on in plant life all around him. The ability to see greatly improves our ability to learn and know. To a large extent seeing is knowing.

In fact, virtually all our knowledge whether regarding plant, animal, or mineral aspects of creation has been gained directly or indirectly as a result of our sight. Our ability to see is only possible because of light, which makes it possible for us to observe and learn about the many miraculous everyday processes around us.

However, the general concepts and principles which we base knowledge upon do not always apply when we consider light. Light performs outside our box of space, time, and matter. According to the theory of relativity, as an object approaches the speed of light, vision is increased. Scientists tell us that if we could reach the speed of light, we could see around corners, and even that which is directly behind us would become visible. Clearly, light is not constrained by time, space, and matter.

The increased vision at the speed of light is a fitting picture of an omniscient God who sees all and knows all. "And there is no creature hidden from His sight, but all things are naked and open to the eyes of Him to whom we must give account" (Hebrews 4:13). The all-knowing God is able to see in ways that we cannot. The speed of light provides extraordinary vision. God is light, and God sees all that is happening in His creation.

Just as all of mankind's knowledge is gained either directly or indirectly because of physical sight, all true spiritual light must come from God who is light. Our spiritual knowledge must come from the One who is all-knowing, "omniscient."

The all-knowing God who sees our every action and knows our every need. He provides a way of receiving His light—a way to have intimate fellowship with Him—and He knows our true reaction to Him.

Sunlight / Sonlight

Sunlight provides physical sight. Sight provides awareness. Awareness allows study and understanding. Understanding our physical surroundings has allowed mankind to make phenomenal discoveries.

Sonlight provides spiritual sight. Sight provides meaning and purpose to our existence. A purposeful life is a meaningful life—a life of intimacy with our Creator.

THINK AND GROW

1. Every living person has physical life. Are you experiencing spiritual life?

2. Do you know personally the all-knowing God?

3. Have you been responsible with the power God has given you? In the home? On the job? In the community? In your fellowships?

4. Look up 1 Chronicles 28:9; Job 37:16; Psalms 94:11, 139:2, 147:4-5; Colossians 2:3; Hebrews 4:13; and 1 John 3:20. How is God's omniscience important to you personally?

10

Seeing the Unseen: Invisible

Imagine with me for a moment that you know someone who has been totally blind since birth. All their knowledge has come through senses other than sight: hearing, smelling, touching, and tasting. Imagine that you are asked by that person to explain light.

How would you explain light to a person who has never seen it? Is there some way you could enable someone to hear light? If a blind person hears the thunder that accompanies lightning, does that allow him to experience light and understand it in the sense that a seeing person does? And what about smelling? The blind person often adapts by acutely developing the functioning senses. But does the ozone odor that accompanies a lightning bolt help to understand light?

Or how about the sense of touch? Someone may touch a cold automobile during the night and then during the heat of midday, but does feeling the warmth created by light produce an understanding of it? Do you know a way to explain light through the sense of taste? There are some effects of light, such as the heat generated by sunlight falling upon our skin, that could readily be understood. But do the effects of light fully explain it? As humans can we see the unseen?

The problem with trying to explain light is that there is nothing tangible about it. We cannot describe what light "feels" like, or even what it "looks" like. There is no way to define light in tangible terms to someone who has not experienced it. About the best we can do is to explain that we recognize light as a sensation that reaches us through our eyes. Although not able to totally understand or explain it, we accept light and its many benefits including life itself and all the beauty that it brings.

As we return to Einstein's theory of relativity, we find that as an object reaches the speed of light, dimensions in the direction of travel become zero. This means that objects traveling at the speed of light become invisible, no matter how large they are at slower speeds. Light defies our normal constraints of spatial dimensions.

Although light is invisible, it is capable of manifesting itself. We can detect the presence of light as it reveals our surroundings, and we discern the effects of light such as feeling its warmth on our skin. It is as if we can see the unseen.

We can utilize the effects of light in many ways. In our era with the use of lasers mankind has harnessed the power of light to perform many wonderful tasks—from supermarket checkout procedures to critical medical operations.

In a similar manner we do not see God, but we see the manifestations of God. The effects of the invisible God are clearly seen. His presence can be known.

The key to understanding either physical or spiritual light is found in observing what it can do. Although no one has ever seen physical light, mankind has learned a great deal about its characteristics; we have applied our knowledge in useful ways.

The effects of Sonlight can be observed also. God has given mankind the Bible, a written description of His dealings with mankind, including insight and statements about His nature and character. If we have spiritual sight, we can apply spiritual truths.

This planet receives its very sustenance for life from invisible light from the sun. God shows us the way to abundant life. The spiritual life possessed by those who understand and trust in God is a source of great invisible power. Those who know God receive great benefits from both the sun and the Son.

The reality of objects becoming invisible at the speed of light is another fitting parallel between sunlight and Sonlight. In Paul's first letter to Timothy we read, "Now to the King eternal, immortal, invisible, to God who alone is wise, be honor and glory forever and ever. Amen" (1 Timothy 1:17). According to the Scriptures, God is invisible.

Sunlight / Sonlight

Sunlight is invisible; however, we can see its effects. Sunlight is practical and useful.

The Son of God for a short period of time was the visible "image of the invisible God" (Colossians 1:15). Sonlight received and acted upon is practical and useful.

THINK AND GROW

1. Have you acknowledged the works of the invisible God?

2. What aspects of God's works are visible?

3. Do you more clearly see the works of God around you than you did a decade ago?

4. Look up 1 Timothy 1:17, Colossians 1:15, Hebrews 11:27, John 1:18, and Romans 1:20. What are the implications for your life of an invisible God?

11

Ultimate Consistency: Immutable

It was a warm day in August and everything was tinder dry. Our family was spending several days at Crater Lake National Park. One morning we hiked up the trail to Garfield Peak. The high-altitude thin air coupled with eighty-degree weather made the hike somewhat tiring. We ate our lunch on top as we gazed upon the glorious panorama of creation below us.

The return trip was equally as tiring due to the steep trail. When we arrived back at our rustic one-room cabin, I sprawled out on a bed.

Suddenly the silence was broken. "Dad, come quick, a fire!" My daughter's voice sounded both excited and frightened. Leaping to the door, I saw a burning piece of wood in the gravel just a foot or so from the wooden steps of the cabin. Linda had a big grin on her face; she was proud of her accomplishment, and I saw the telltale magnifying glass in her hand. She had managed to concentrate the sun's energy onto a small area of the wood, causing it to burst into flame.

Our sun is continuously using vast quantities of energy. According to Einstein's formula, the sun uses more than four million tons of matter each and every second.

Consider the awesome size of the universe. Some stars may have ceased to exist millions of years ago, yet that may not be known for millions more years to come. The reason for this is that while traveling at over 186,000 miles per second, light may take millions of years to reach our planet from distant stars. The light we see when we look into the nighttime heavens is old light, very old light. Light does not lose its energy in all those millions of years. It is unchanging and represents the ultimate in consistency.

The theory of relativity has helped mankind to understand the remarkably consistent and unchanging character of the physical laws of nature. It demonstrates that physical life would not be possible without the consistent orderliness of our physical laws. On the basis of the three different theories that enable us to understand the behavior of light, we are able to predict its performance and have learned to trust that it will perform tomorrow as it has in the past and does today. Light has an unchanging and trustworthy nature.

A remarkable implication of Einstein's theory is that no matter how fast or in which direction we were to travel in an imaginary spaceship, light would always travel past us at the same speed. Even if we traveled toward a light source at nine-tenths' the speed of light, any light passing us in either direction would be going by us at 186,000 miles per second relative to us. This is another indication of the absoluteness of the nature of light.

This unchanging nature of physical light is a picture of the unchanging nature of Sonlight. The unchanging, "immutable" God is an absolute God. "Jesus Christ is the same yesterday, today, and forever" (Hebrews 13:8).

With our human tendencies toward constant change, it is difficult to perceive that God could be absolute and unchanging. Nevertheless, from His Word we know that He has no variableness.

"Every good gift and every perfect gift is from above, and cometh down from the Father of lights, with whom is no variableness, neither shadow of turning" (James 1:17 kjv). Think about one aspect of this verse. No light ever has a shadow! Shadows appear behind objects which light shines upon.

He has given us spiritual laws in His Word, the Bible. They are as consistent and unchanging as physical laws. God is immutable, that is, He is unchanging (see for example Malachi 3:6).

Sunlight / Sonlight

Sunlight displays a remarkably consistent, unchanging nature which is hard for our human minds to fully grasp.

Sonlight displays a remarkably consistent, unchanging nature which is hard for our human minds to fully grasp.

THINK AND GROW

1. I am sure that you have learned to trust and rely upon physical light because of the consistency of its behavior. God does not change. Have you learned to confidently and consistently trust Him based upon His unchanging nature?

2. There are some passages in the Old Testament that state that God changed His mind. How can those passages be understood in light of His unchanging nature?

12

Without Time Constraints: Immortal

How long has it been since you contemplated the little pump inside of you? You are dependent upon your heart for your very life. Each minute your heart beats approximately seventy times. In one-hour your little blood pump forces 4,200 squirts of blood through your blood ways.

Your circulatory system stretches over 10,000 miles in length as it weaves its way throughout your body. In one day, just twenty-four hours, your heart beats 100,800 times, and in a year well over thirty-six million times. Your very survival is dependent upon your little heart, which is only about the size of your fist and weighs about half a pound. If you should live seventy years, your heart will total over two and a half billion individual beats.

In one-year the volume of blood pumped will be about 650,000 gallons, or enough to fill 81 railroad tank cars of 8,000 gallons each. Each of those tank cars would weigh about 65 tons, yet the energy generated by your heart in just twelve hours is equivalent to the energy required to raise one of those 65-ton railroad cars one foot off the ground. It is no wonder that the psalmist could say, "I will praise You, for I am fearfully and wonderfully made" (Psalm 139:14).

Yet there is one fact that we must deal with, and that is the fact that we are mortal beings. While it is true that we are marvelously complex creatures, it is also true that from the time of our first heartbeat we are in the process of aging, and therefore dying. All living things have a life span. For some insects it may be measured in days, hours, or even minutes. For some trees it may be hundreds of years. But all living things have a finite life span.

From the moment we are born, we begin to die. Although our opinion about life and death is powerless to change the reality about death, realization of these sobering thoughts may have some positive rewards. Dedication to living the remainder of our lives to the fullest is one way that we might react. Desire followed by action to make one's life count for all eternity is a positive step that can be taken.

As we return to the theory of relativity, we find that aging slows down as an object approaches the speed of light. Scientists tell us that this is not just a perception but a reality. A ten-year-old child who sets off on a continuous journey of one hundred years at 99 percent of the speed of light would end the journey as a 24-year-old. In other words, the aging process would have slowed to only one-seventh of the normal aging process. This person would look like, act like, and would literally be (remember, time slows down) a 24-year-old. Another person born the same day would be 110 years old if still living.

At 100 percent of the speed of light, time ceases and our normal time constraints have been removed.

In the Book of Genesis, we read that on the first day of the creation week, God caused light to appear (Genesis 1:3). Later in the New Testament we read that God commanded light to shine out of darkness (2 Corinthians 4:6). Notice that Scripture does not say God created light. Is this an indication of the eternal nature of light?

Again, we see a fitting symbol of God. At the speed of light, time has ceased to be. God's Word tells us that God is immortal. "Until our Lord Jesus Christ's appearing, which He will manifest in His own time, He who is the blessed and only Potentate, the King of kings and Lord of lords, who alone has immortality, dwelling in unapproachable light, whom no man has seen or can see" (1 Timothy 6:14-16). Most importantly, God allows us to inherit eternal life. We can be "partakers of the divine nature" (2 Peter 1:4). One of the characteristics of God's divine nature is immortality.

Sunlight / Sonlight

Sunlight has an ongoing life beyond anything else we can observe.

Sonlight has an ongoing life which is absolute without any decay or deterioration.

THINK AND GROW

1. God is immortal and He imparts eternal life to those who place their trust in Him. Have you come out of the shadows into the divine life, and are you a participant in God's nature?

2. Look up 1 Timothy 1:17, 6:16; Daniel 7:14; and Isaiah 40:28. Why is the immortality of God significant?

3. Look up 2 Peter 1:4 and Hebrews 3:14, 6:4. List the implications of these verses with regards to your life.

13

Uniquely Unique: Holy

Have you ever experienced the total blackness that is present deep inside a cave? Our family had a tradition of spending a week every summer at Sunriver in the central part of Oregon. Each year while at that resort we would force ourselves away from the enjoyment we found at the resort to take at least one side trip in the surrounding area outside Sunriver. The year our daughter Laura was two years old our trip was to the Lava River Caves.

Laura was riding on my back in a backpack as we descended into the cool cave. Six-year-old Linda clutched her mother's hand as we entered this underground world. While still near the entrance I lit our propane camp lantern and we made a double-check of our back-up flashlight.

About a mile from the entrance we approached the end of the easily explored cave. The cave had been becoming smaller and smaller so that by the time we reached the end, we were crawling along a narrow low passage. We decided to provide our children with the unique feeling of utter blackness that we had experienced several times in other caves.

We prepared them by explaining what we were going to do and the length of time that there would be no light. Being confident we had a good hold on each of them, the lantern was turned off.

After a couple of minutes our girls instinctively realized that their eyes were not going to "dark adapt" and that this darkness was for real! The complete darkness of such an experience is difficult to describe to anyone who has not experienced it.

Our children were quite silent, and we attempted to keep the talk going in order to reduce their fears. When I struck a match to relight the lantern, it was as if a large electric light had been switched on; a small match illuminated the entire area. We all marveled at the amount of light from a single match; then we started our return trip.

Not much more was said by either Linda or Laura until we were about three-quarters of the way out of the cave. Then Laura, once again riding in the backpack, said, "Big dark!" From that point back to the car, there was constant discussion among the four of us about what has since been known to us as "the big dark."

Without any light for any substantial period of time, one cannot help but have a feeling of hopelessness and despair, but given the light from even a single match, hope and vitality are immediately present. And as we have so often said, light and life are so closely linked to each other.

Our environment is constrained by time, space, and matter. Other environments are different. Consider for example that outer space is full of light yet is very dark! Light is constantly traveling through space in many directions. All the natural light that we receive on earth has come to us through space. Yet we know that it is very dark in outer space. This is an interesting fact in light of Old Testament statements such as, "The Lord said that He would dwell in the thick darkness" (1 Kings 8:12 kjv). The God who is light dwells in darkness!

While light and darkness can coexist in outer space, that is not true on earth. Light will always dispel darkness in our environment. As we consider light and darkness within the constraints of our environment, we find that they are mutually exclusive.

The Apostle John in his gospel and his first epistle says a great deal about life, love, and light. This trio is an interesting and enlightening description of the very nature of God—since there cannot be a diluting or mixing of opposites.

Darkness represents death; light provides life. Something cannot be full of life and be dead at the same time. Such a state of being is impossible. Where life reigns, death has no existence. Where death reigns, there is no life.

It is also true that real love and hate are mutually exclusive. One cannot love and hate the same thing. God loves the sinner while He simultaneously hates sin, but it would be an incorrect understanding of Scripture to think God loves and hates the sinner. It would also be incorrect to think that God could hate and love sin. Neither can we sincerely love and hate our fellow man.

Light and darkness do not mingle. The reality that light and dark cannot coexist in the same physical area on earth is a wonderful picture of the absolute holy nature of God. His light is available to all who believe, yet His nature remains undefiled. While on earth, God in flesh mingled with publicans and all manner of sinners yet remained the pure, spotless Lamb of God. The pure nature of light is another parallel that shows us the nature of God who is light.

We have said that the spiritual light from God brings man out of his spiritual darkness, "to open their eyes, in order to turn them from darkness to light, and from the power of Satan to God, that they may receive forgiveness of sins" (Acts 26:18). God offers spiritual light and sight to those who are willing to truly seek Him.

As believers, those who have received eternal life, we are to live holy lives. "As He who called you is holy, you also be holy in all your conduct, because it is written, *Be holy, for I am holy*" (1 Peter 1:15-16). Wherever there is genuine spiritual life, darkness can no longer be. God has called us to be children of light.

Sunlight / Sonlight

Of all substances and phenomena known to man, sunlight is unique and totally surprising in its properties.

The Son of God is uniquely unique!

THINK AND GROW

1. List the ways God is unique. Make it as complete as possible.

2. Do you stand out as a reflection of God's uniqueness to commonness around you?

3. God's holiness is seen in Isaiah 6:3, Revelation 4:8, Habakkuk 1:13, 1 Peter 1:15-16, and other passages. How would you explain God's holiness to a small child?

14

True Perpetual Motion: Self-Existent

Like many people, I enjoy good food. I especially like to go out to a fine restaurant with my wife or with friends and enjoy a time of fellowship around the table. Have you ever considered how different our lives would be if we did not have to eat? But eat we must! But why do we eat?

Our bodies derive necessary energy for survival from the food that we eat. Horses eat their hay and their oats. We put gasoline into our cars to provide the energy to propel us down our highways. We live in an energy-conscious age and are becoming increasingly more sensitive to the amount of energy we use and the way in which we use it.

The universe runs on energy. The great ocean liner the Queen Mary propelled itself thirteen feet forward for each gallon of fuel consumed; and maybe for a ship that weighed in excess of eighty thousand tons and pushed a depth of thirty-nine feet of water aside at a speed of 30 knots, that's not too bad. But thirteen feet per gallon is over 400 gallons per mile.

The first space shuttle, Columbia, consumed approximately eight tons of fuel per second during lift-off. This is approximately equivalent to the fuel consumed by 25 fully loaded 747 jumbo jets. We live in an age of energy consumption, and we have been told there is an energy crisis.

We have seen previously that the sun is giving off vast quantities of energy. But we must be careful to note that because of the vast size of our star, it is for practical purposes remaining unchanged, that is, it does not require constant refueling. "We may say that each square

81

inch of the sun's surface is only losing about a twentieth of an ounce a century."[8]

Compared to man's frame of reference and time scales, the sun, our source of physical light, is self-existing. It has no need of external refueling.

While we live in an energy-conscious age, we are also great consumers of energy. Provision of suitable sources of energy is becoming a worldwide concern. The sun, the ultimate supplier of all our energy, is giving off vast quantities of energy. Even so, by any human time standard, the sun is in no need of refueling.

The amount of energy being given off by the sun is of little consequence because of its enormous size. The sun is perhaps changing slower than anything else that we can possibly observe. Even though the sun is giving off vast amounts of energy, it will take a period of about two billion years for it to lose one seven-thousandth of its total matter.[9] "The lifetime of a human being is measured in decades; the lifetime of the sun is a hundred million times longer."[10]

For all practical purposes the sun symbolizes true perpetual motion.

In a universe where everything is dependent upon something else in order to exist, the sun is the most self-existent object that could be used for analogy to a self-existent God. (The theological term is "aseity.")

When we contemplate the majesty and uniqueness of the self-existent God, it should humble us. He has given us a written record, the Holy Bible, so that we may learn of Him. John in three words, "God is light," provides us a profound image of the self-existent God of the cosmos.

Sunlight / Sonlight

Sunlight exists without the need for care, maintenance, or refueling.

Sonlight is self-existing without the need of any outside resources.

THINK AND GROW

1. Have you humbled yourself before God and acknowledged that your very existence is dependent upon the Self-Existent One?

2. What role do you think God's self-existence plays with respect to His eternal nature?

15

Evidence That Speaks for Itself: Self-Manifest

We receive light in many forms every day. One winter morning on my way to work I found myself driving over an overpass at dawn. Ahead of me loomed majestic cloud formations painted in the most exquisite shades of reds and purples. It was the most beautiful sunrise I had ever witnessed. I longed for my camera so that I could share the moment with others.

As I dropped down off the overpass and turned toward the right, I entered a flat farming area. By the time I reached an old weather-scarred farmhouse, there was a low ground fog that completely obscured the sunrise. The sunrise was still there in all its beauty and I'm sure that it was still visible from the overpass vantage point, but it took direct undiffused sunlight to bring out all of the beauty.

Light allows us to see beauty. The beauty is there all along, but light allows us to see it! In fact, it is only because of light that we are able to see anything at all. Even the diffused sunlight in the fog allowed me to see my surroundings. Without light we have no sight at all. The most basic characteristic of light is that it allows us to see.

In Romans we read "... what may be known about God is plain to them, because God has made it plain to them. For since the creation of the world God's invisible qualities—His eternal power and divine nature—have been clearly seen, being understood from what has been made, so that men are without excuse" (Romans 1:19-20 niv). The evidence speaks for itself.

It is only light that makes the beauty of creation visible. Sunlight allows us to see nature. Sonlight allows us to begin to comprehend God.

It is light that makes vision possible. Light manifests that which is already there. God is light. Physical light allows us to have physical sight. Spiritual light allows us to have spiritual sight. Just as physical objects are made visible by physical light, so even the thoughts and intents of our hearts are made visible by spiritual light.

In a philosophical sense, light is a force. In fact, light exerts about 30 pounds of pressure per square mile on earth.

Illumination and heat do not travel through space from the sun to our earth. If they did, outer space would be very bright and very hot, just the opposite of what we know to be true. The presence of light is made evident as it strikes an object, producing illumination and heat.

God is light. As the spiritual light from God touches individuals, it reveals the truth about their inner selves. As Sonlight reaches individuals, it causes a friction, a restlessness, a sort of spiritual heat.

As beings made in the image of God, we are to reflect His image, and we find our only true fulfillment in relationship to the Creator. Until that relationship exists, a deep, yet subtle restlessness continues in the soul of the individual.

Sunlight / Sonlight

Sunlight is not a physical material according to our normal ways of defining objects. We can see the effects of sunlight all around us.

The Son of God is spirit (John 4:24) and is "outside our box" of normal thinking. We can see the effects of Sonlight all around us.

THINK AND GROW

1. How is light reflecting your inner beauty?

2. Other than light, what is self-manifest because of its effects rather than our ability to see it directly? List as many as you can but include at least one natural and one spiritual.

3. Look up Luke 12:2-3, John 3:19-20, Ephesians 5:14, and Romans 1:18-20. From these verses what is one of the key things that light does?

16

Under Absolute Control: Sovereign

Many games are played with dice. What are the chances on any single roll of the dice of any specific number coming up? A die, one of a pair of dice, is a cube, hence has six equal sides. It contains from one to six dots on each of its six sides. Each of the numbers from one to six is represented on one side, therefore no number occurs on more than one side. There is one chance out of six that any specific side will be on top at the end of a roll.

Adding a second die changes the odds. A seven can result through six different combinations (1+6, 2+5, 3+4, 4+3, 5+2, and 6+1), and the chances are six out of thirty-six, or one out of six.

Similarly, we can easily calculate the odds for other numbers with two dice. For example, the chance of rolling a two is only one out of thirty-six. This is because the only way to obtain a two is by rolling a one on both dice.

Even in a "game of chance" there is order. Because of this order, the results of a large number of dice rolls are very predictable. This is, of course, the basis of assured profitability for the gaming industry.

There are ten distinct numbers in our numbering system. We could put ten slips of paper into a basket, each representing one of those numbers, and then randomly withdraw a number or sequence of numbers. The chances of drawing the number one on the first try would be one out of ten. The probability of drawing one on the first try and then two on the second try would be one out of ninety! To withdraw 1-2-3 in sequence would have a probability of one out of seven hundred twenty.

The probability of withdrawing numbers one through ten in numerical sequence would be equivalent to one chance out of 3,628,800.

Incidentally, if instead of ten slips of paper from which to draw we had a very large number of slips of paper, with the numbers one through ten still equally proportioned, the chances of drawing one through ten in sequence would be only a little greater than one out of 10,000,000,000.

Would you believe me if I said that nobody wrote the material you are reading—it just happened? Well in a sense someone did not write this material. It is made up of twenty-six letters that we call our alphabet. The writer did not create that alphabet; the writer just arranged the sequence of the letters!

Everything that was necessary to create this written material has existed for a long time. We know the alphabet has been around for a long time. There is really nothing new presented in this material. The fact is that the twenty-six letters of the alphabet and the ten numbers are all that are required.

The missing necessary ingredient is an orderly and meaningful arrangement of the letters and numbers. A great deal of thought, planning, and hard work is necessary. Samuel Johnson once said, "what is written without effort is in general read without pleasure."

In view of probabilities, no one would really believe that a book could come into existence without an author. One may disagree with the logic or organization that an author has used, but that does not deny the existence of the author.

Observing the complexity of the natural world all around us, how can we deny the existence of the supreme author? God is the "author of life" (Acts 3:15 niv) and the "author and finisher of our faith" (Hebrews 12:2). The revelation of nature is sufficient to cause a person to believe in the supreme author-creator.

The Bible tells us that God has created all things. It is difficult for finite minds to comprehend the God who could create this beautiful universe out of nothing, yet when we study closely the beauty all around us, we discover that all of nature is primarily nothing. Everything is made up of atoms. Physical matter is similar to outer space—vast areas of nothingness punctuated with occasional objects with much smaller objects orbiting around them. What we think of as solid material is really miniature little solar systems of atomic particles.

"The electrons move around their orbits about seven thousand million times in a millionth of a second, and we should expect endless collision and hopeless chaos, there is instead the beauty and rest of perfect symmetry."[11]

The parallel is clear. The Scriptures tell us that God is light and that by Him all things consist (Colossians 1:15-17). The great designer and controller is sovereign. He is in absolute control. "The lot is cast into the lap, but its every decision is from the Lord" (Proverbs 16:33). God has given us a free will to choose how much we walk in His light. True beauty and harmony is the result of allowing the light of God to fully shine on our lives.

Man is able to look at the atomic structure of all materials and determine what any substance is made of through the analysis of light in a process called Spectrum Analysis. There is a spiritual parallel here. If we are in God's light, we will reflect His light to those around us. Since we are fashioned after God, we have a resident beauty within us of being like God. As others look at us, they see the resident beauty of God reflected by us.

There is another lesson for us as we consider the basic emptiness of all matter. We are literally hollow men. God provides for our lives real meaning and purpose, giving us the abundant life. God is sovereign. He reigns in absolute control. Denying His existence or denying His sovereignty does not change the facts any more than denying the atomic structure of material changes its composition. The Bible declares God's absolute control over the universe that He created.

Sunlight / Sonlight

Sunlight reveals the vast complexity of our physical surroundings. A thoughtful person cannot begin to comprehend all the aspects of the grand design all around us. Science has helped us understand some of the basics.

Sonlight reveals the vast complexity of the spiritual world. A thoughtful person cannot begin to comprehend all the spiritual forces and realities around us. The Word of God—both His written Word and His living Word (Jesus Christ), is God's communication to mankind providing us insight into the basics.

THINK AND GROW

1. The question is not, "Will you humble yourself before God"—that will happen in the future for sure. Rather, the question is, "To this point in your life how much have you humbled yourself before the Sovereign of the universe?"

2. When adversity enters your life, do you look past the messenger and understand God's love? Have you learned to refuse to look at second causes and understand God's role in allowing the rain to fall in your life?

3. Look up Acts 17:25, 28; Colossians 1:16-17; Ephesians 1:11; Daniel 7:14; Proverbs 16:33; and Isaiah 46:9b-11. From these verses how would you define the sovereignty of God?

17

Without Full Understanding

I am awakened by the alarm clock in the early morning. Without much consideration I assume that it is five a.m.—the time that I set the alarm the night before. Reaching for the light switch, I expect the power to flow to the light bulb and the room to be illuminated with man-made light without any problems. Brushing my teeth, I have confidence that my toothpaste is not contaminated with any harmful substance. Life is too complicated to worry about or study every aspect of my daily life. What worked yesterday I anticipate will work today.

For breakfast I enjoy my favorite granola, adding milk produced and processed by people I have never met. A slice of my special bread from a local bakery and fruit which may have come from many different parts of the world complete my breakfast. Seldom do I give the safety of these routine actions any consideration.

The sun rises in the east and the Creator-made light arrives just as it did yesterday and the day before.

Driving to work without a concern, I cross over the large Interstate 205 bridge across the Columbia River—it was structurally engineered by civil engineers. I trust they knew what they were doing when they designed the bridge. Over the years the bridge was being built, the workmen followed the specifications exactly—at least I assume they did. I do not have the education to assure me the engineers did their jobs perfectly. Even if I did, I have no access to their specifications or drawings. I have learned to trust the I-205 bridge since every day without fail it has allowed thousands of vehicles to pass over to the other side.

On our spiritual journeys some individuals stumble over the idea of "faith." They have no problem sitting in a chair and trusting it to hold them. Faith, or trust, in the spiritual realm is no different than in the natural realm. Based on personal experience or the observed experiences of others, we are willing to cross the bridge.

Years ago, as a young boy in a Sunday school class, I heard a reportedly true story which I have never forgotten. A tight-wire walker had set up his wire across Niagara Falls and a large crowd sat in bleachers on both sides. The crowd anxiously watched as he slowly made his way across the treacherous waterfall—carefully utilizing the long balancing rod he carried.

After making a roundtrip he asked the crowd, "How many of you think I could push a wheelbarrow across to the other side?" The crowd was hushed; then one, and another began shouting, "I do!" He took his wheelbarrow, with its special cupped wheel, and again slowly, with anxious moments, made his way across and back again.

Now the tight-wire artist raised the ante. "How many of you think I could do this again, but this time with two 90-pound sacks of cement in the wheelbarrow?" This time, based on what had been witnessed, the majority of the crowd soon began cheering and shouting, "Yes!" He loaded the wheelbarrow and started across.

Once again, as in the two previous efforts, there were a number of anxious moments. Eventually he made his way all the way across and back.

Now he asked another question. "How many believe I could replace those two sacks of cement with a person and make it across and back?" By now the crowd had witnessed enough that they were into it. Almost instantaneously the entire crowd erupted with, "We believe! We believe!"

This time the artist looked directly at the crowd for a few moments until a hush came over them. His eyes began to rove and then locked in on a gentleman seated in the third row—one of the most boisterous of the respondents. "You! Get into the wheelbarrow."

At this, the man rose, carefully moved to the front of the crowd, turned to his right, away from the artist, and took off running.

Faith is not an emotion or feeling. True faith requires a confidence. Just as in the physical realm, intellectual belief alone without action is not the type of faith—trust—required in our spiritual journeys.

The person who must "have *all* the answers" before acting will always be on the sidelines unwilling to act.

Sunlight / Sonlight

Sunlight and its effects upon our earth are truly amazing. It takes a huge amount of faith to accept some of the scientific concepts related to sunlight which have been revealed in previous chapters.

Sonlight and His effects upon mankind are truly amazing. It takes faith to accept some of the spiritual realities laid out for us in the God-breathed living Word of God.

THINK AND GROW

Can you think of situation from your experience where someone to their detriment failed to act in a timely fashion because they were waiting for more answers?

18

Three Parameters: Trinity

We have experienced the past, we live in the present, and we anticipate living in the future. It is the combination of the three aspects of time that constitute life—except at the instant of conception or death.

We live in a three-dimensional environment (width, length, and height). Without all three dimensions there can be no matter.

The three aspects of time and the three dimensions that define a material object are just two examples of how the concept of three aspects of one item is common in our thinking. You cannot visualize an object unless there are three dimensions or fully understand an individual without knowing something of their background, their current situation, and their plans, hopes, and dreams for the future.

There are several ways that light manifests a triune nature. In order to explain this three-part nature, scientists have developed three distinct theories to comprehend light's behavior. Geometric optics explains the straight-line behavior of light; wave optics deals with the wave nature or electromagnetic character of light; and quantum optics is necessary to explain the energy levels of light.

In both the subtractive and the additive processes of color sensation, there are three primary colors, from which we can obtain the full gamut of colors. As school children learn, any color must be obtained by some combination of the three primary colors.

In order to technically describe any color, three parameters must be defined. Luminous flux describes the power, or brightness of a color. Dominant wavelength describes the hue, or main characteristics of a color. Finally, purity defines the saturation, or richness of a specific color. It is important to note that all three characteristics must be defined in order to fully describe any particular color.

There is also the reality that visible light is but a small band of the total electromagnetic spectrum, the entire group of waves which are related to electric and magnetic fields. Scientists often refer to the regions in the spectrum above and below visible light as light. Certainly, the entire electromagnetic spectrum is one phenomenon.

Composing the spectrum are three major sections: infrared, an invisible portion of light (below red), visible light, and ultraviolet, another invisible portion of light (beyond violet).

Other trios which figure prominently in the study of light include the three reactions of light to an object, the three classifications of light sources which scientists use, and the three parameters in equations dealing with geometric optics.[12] All of these are worthy of further study.

While light has aspects that are puzzling, even baffling, on the basis of the three different theories, we are able to understand many aspects of light and its behavior. Mankind has learned to utilize that knowledge in useful and productive ways.

The three-in-one aspect of spiritual light includes the source (Father), the motion or activity (Holy Spirit), and the manifestation of God on earth (the Son). Understanding the eternal Father (beyond time), the invisible working of the Holy Spirit (beyond space), and the life on earth of Jesus Christ (visible in matter), enables us to understand God who is Light.

We are able to understand the nature and ways of light as we reason outside the limitations of time, space, and matter. In much the same way, we can begin to really understand God, His nature, and His ways by looking outside these limitations.

Is it any wonder that the Bible portrays the Creator as a three-dimensional God?

Sunlight / Sonlight

There are a number of sets or groups of three which enable us to understand Sunlight.

Sonlight, Jesus Christ, is one member of a triune God.

THINK AND GROW

1. Three-in-one concepts are commonplace in science. Why do you think the concept of a three-in-one God is difficult for human minds to accept?

2. Why do you think it is difficult to trust God?

19

Clearly Visible

Many of us question the reality of God when we, or those we are close to, experience the deep troubles of life. We all experience troubles during our lifetimes. Earnest Hemmingway stated, "Life breaks us all."

In the early days of space exploration one of the Russian cosmonauts returned from space and matter-of-factly stated that he hadn't seen God! The essence of his comment was, "I've been there, done that, I didn't see God—therefore there is no God."

Because God was not seen by Russian cosmonauts or our own astronauts, does that mean that God does not exist? Does it mean that He is absent from outer space? Or, is He present but invisible?

We know that it is dark, very dark, in outer space. We also are aware that outer space is full of light traveling from stars in all directions. Only a tiny fraction of this light travels in a direction that causes it to reach our planet earth. Space travelers do not see the light that is so abundant in space.

The Scriptures tell us that the God who *is* light dwells in darkness! (Examples include 2 Chronicles 6:1, 1 Kings 8:12, 2 Samuel 22:10-12, and Psalm 18:9-11.) It is also clear from the Biblical account of Moses receiving the Ten Commandments that God dwells in darkness (for example Exodus 20:21 and Deuteronomy 4:11, 5:23).

In the middle of his extreme trials, Job understood that the God who is light dwells in darkness (Job 38:19-21 and others). There are other examples throughout Scripture.

We have previously seen that light passes any object, in either direction, at a *relative* speed of about 186,000 miles per second. This is an absolute. If we could build a space ship that could travel through space at 185,900 miles per second and it was on a parallel course with light traveling in the same direction, the speed of light as it overtook our space ship would still be 186,000 miles per second faster than we were traveling!

And if light were coming toward us while we were traveling at the same 185,900 miles per second, the difference in speed as that light passed by would still be 186,000 miles per second! The speed of light is an absolute with regard to all material objects. This is one of the many remarkable implications of Einstein's widely accepted little formula. Light is truly unapproachable.

We are told that God is unapproachable and cannot be seen (by astronauts or anyone else), "Who alone is immortal and Who lives in unapproachable light, Whom no one has seen or can see" (1 Timothy 6:16 niv).

We have also seen that sunlight and Sonlight are not unique in having a three-part nature. Our created environment is confined by space that is measured by three physical dimensions—length, width, and height. As humans, we are confined by time, space, and matter. But our physical constraints do not affect light.

Therefore, to begin to comprehend spiritual light, we must move outside our human constraints of time, space, and matter. We must be capable of flexibility in how we think, reason, and perceive.

The belief in a triune God is puzzling to many. But man can better understand God by looking at His three distinct personalities. All three personalities must be taken into account in order to fully understand God in a meaningful way.

God is described in Scripture with the same characteristics that describe light. God is not limited to time, space, or matter. He has no beginning or end, is ever-present, all-powerful, self-existent, and invisible.

We are better able to understand physical light when we consider the sun as our light source, the waves and packets as the energy and motion of light, and our material environment as the visible display of the presence of light. We can better relate to the God who is light by observing His three personalities.

The Father might be likened to the source of our physical light, the sun. The Father characterizes unapproachable light and all of light's amazing attributes.

The Holy Spirit might be considered the motion, or energetic flow aspect of God. There is a parallel with the waves and packets of physical light, which describe the motion and flow characteristics of the sun's light. As the sun creates the action and motion that is seen and felt on earth, so also the action and motion of the Spirit of God is felt and seen in our lives. Just as the sun hardens clay and melts butter, individuals respond differently to the Spirit of God.

Jesus Christ, the Son of God, is God in time, space, and matter. He makes it possible for mankind to see and better understand God, presenting God in human flesh—relatable—God made clearly visible. Now we have an aspect of God we can see!

As with any three-in-one, none of the parts is a fullness of the complete whole, nor is the complete whole fully comprehended without each part. We see the visual aspect of light, yet we understand that this visual aspect is only a part of light. Visible light, as we have seen, is only one of three parts of the entire electromagnetic spectrum. Jesus Christ, God visible on earth, is only one of the three personalities of God. He brings into relatable visibility the attributes of the entire Triune One.

As a person and his word are considered one, so the spoken Word of God is considered as God Himself. "In the beginning was the Word, and the Word was with God, and the Word was God" (John 1:1). Jesus is the visible "Word" of God.

Humanity sees evidence of light and understand many of its characteristics by observing the color variances of material substances that absorb and reflect light. In the same way, as we observe the life of Jesus Christ on earth, we are able to more fully understand the nature and ways of God. "He who has seen Me, has seen the Father" (John 14:9). Jesus Christ on earth is the visible Light of the World (Matthew 5:14; John 8:12, 9:5).

In the life of Jesus Christ, mankind is able to visualize God in our world of time, space, and matter. The period of time when the Son of God walked on earth is the great time divide in mankind's history. Time for mankind is marked by two distinct periods: B.C. (before Christ) and A.D., the period of time after Jesus Christ walked on earth.

Sunlight and Sonlight have similar amazing characteristics. Perhaps one of the most intriguing aspects of both is the way mankind tends to take them for granted. The astronauts did not see God in space. They didn't see the light that was passing through space either, but we know it was there in abundance. Today we receive daily benefits from sunlight and Sonlight, seldom giving either a serious thought.

"The heavens declare the glory of God; and the firmament shows His handiwork. Day unto day utters speech, and night unto night reveals knowledge. There is no speech nor language where their voice is not heard. Their line has gone out through all the earth, and their words to the end of the world. In them He has set a tabernacle for the sun, which is like a bridegroom coming out of his chamber and rejoices like a strong man to run its race. Its rising is from one end of heaven, and its circuit to the other end; and there is nothing hidden from its heat" (Psalm 19:1-6).

~ *Quote* ~ "What the sun is to the day, what the moon is to the night, what the dew is to the flower, such is Jesus Christ to us."—Charles H. Spurgeon

Sunlight / Sonlight

Sunlight is all around us and yet we do not see light. We believe in light because of the effects which we observe.

God is pervasive in the affairs of mankind. He has even given us His written Word. Christians believe in Sonlight because of His effects which can be observed and the inner reality which can be experienced.

THINK AND GROW

When do you think it would be easier to visualize God, before Christ was born or after He had come to earth and ascended back to heaven?

COMPLEX
Yet
SIMPLE!

20

Mysteriously Complex

The study of the nature of light is now a fundamental activity of science. However, as late as three hundred years ago scientists were still arguing about whether light appeared instantaneously or traveled at some tremendous speed. It was during the late 1930s that the speed and behavior of light became immensely important to scientists.

Einstein's theories of relativity have not only increased our understanding of light but have allowed many of the great technological advances of our times. The rapid rate of change in our "high-tech" society is only possible because of our understanding of natural light.

Light is essential to our daily existence. It is the energy source for all plants and animals. Without the sunlight that bathes our planet, there could be no life on earth.

A Smithsonian publication has this to say about the importance of sunlight: "Everything that happens, from rainbows to the fall of sparrows, from snow to the winds that let us sail or fly, from the appearance of civilizations to their demise in the sands of time—all is dependent on our star."[13] The essential light of the world is the sun.

Perhaps the most succinct statement about the importance of light is that light makes vision possible. It is light that reveals the world of beauty and color. All of mankind's knowledge of his world is based upon his observations. The vast majority of these observations would be impossible without light.

If it were not for an analysis of the light that comes to us from distant galaxies, we would know virtually nothing about the universe. A primary benefit that we receive from light is in its ability to reveal, to make vision possible.

Even today light is largely a mystery to man. It is mysteriously complex. The more we have learned about it, the more marvelous and mysterious it has become. Einstein wrote, "The most beautiful thing we can experience is the mysterious. It is the source of all true art and science."[14]

No one, not even Einstein, has ever fully understood light, but we have learned that the nature of light is absolute and therefore predictable.

The atomic structure of materials is a key to mankind's future. We now know that chemistry, electricity, and light are all related to atomic structure. Life and light are related. With just about one hundred different naturally occurring elements, our world is made up of a vast array of plants, animals, and minerals. No two human beings, no two trees, and no two geological formations are identical.

The interrelationship of life and light is very complex. The interrelationship of matter, energy, light, and life is a great mystery of the universe. "Something deeply hidden had to be behind things," according to Einstein.[15]

Sunlight / Sonlight

Sunlight was little understood until relatively recent history. Few doubt the existence of sunlight even though science continues to remain baffled by some aspects of light. A core benefit of sunlight is its ability to reveal by allowing physical vision.

Sonlight is little understood by a significant portion of mankind. Some doubt the existence of a designer for this complex and vast creation which continues to amaze us. A core benefit of Sonlight is His ability to reveal by allowing spiritual vision.

THINK AND GROW

1. Do you regularly acknowledge spiritual light as essential for your daily living?

2. Have you allowed the light of God's Word to reveal to you the inner secrets of your life and true motivations?

21

A Common Simplicity

While on the one hand matter and life are very complex, there is a commonalty among all things—a common simplicity. Virtually everything is made up of nothing.

For instance, analyze a piece of gold magnified a billion times. Each atom would at this magnification be about two feet in diameter. Virtually all the mass (weight) of each atom is concentrated in the nucleus, and at this magnification the nucleus would be only about one-thousandth of an inch in diameter. This very small nucleus is surrounded by even tinier electrons that are moving about very rapidly at speeds close to that of light.[16]

All matter is in a similar way made up of atoms, which are mostly nothing, and we know that light, or energy, and matter are in a sense only different forms of the same thing.

The chemical structure of all matter, the electrical nature of all matter, and the electromagnetic spectrum are woven together. All life processes are accompanied by electrical phenomena. Electricity is a sign of life. Every living thing is a source of electricity. The complexity we call life is woven together with light in intricate ways.

The more man learns, the more the complexities of our environment are revealed, but at the same time a simplification is occurring. Currently much scientific inquiry and research is seeking to develop a common explanation of our natural environment under one comprehensive theory rather than the several basic theories necessary today.

For decades scientists have been searching for a single theory which could explain everything. In recent years there has been much publicity about String Theory. Another common single theory is M Theory. But while many believe in a common simplicity, there is no denying the overall complexity. Some String Theory scientists have estimated that there might be 10^{500} possible solutions—that is a huge number! The popular scientific media loves to portray new theories as the greatest thing since sliced bread—or should we say since Einstein. But to date no significant progress has been made with regard to a one size fits all theory.

Meanwhile chemistry is becoming more like physics. Biology is becoming more like chemistry. Even areas such as behavioral science are becoming more like biology.

We are making some strides toward a unified understanding of all of nature.

The astronomer is learning that his science is becoming more and more like the science of the particle physicist who is dealing with the planetary orbits of the very tiny.

I believe that deeply hidden are secrets yet to be discovered which show the unified nature of all of creation.

There are those who believe that there is no purpose to this world of ours, that human life has no more meaning than does a grain of sand upon the beach. Man, some believe, has evolved to his powerful wisdom merely by chance. The human eye evolved together with the brain to provide vision. Is this the reality of man's existence?

Those who have difficulty in believing in the Creator of the universe must ask what it is, if not God, which keeps the delicate balance of all things under control. The more scientists learn about the order and intricacies of our environment, the more we realize how remarkably consistent and marvelous the laws of science really are.

Assume for a moment that all of life as we know it today evolved from a "big bang" some fifteen billion years ago. One obvious question relates to what existed to cause the big bang? And secondly, where did it come from?

Aside from those questions, however, it takes an incredible amount of faith to believe that the remarkable scientific facts, delicate balance of nature, and astonishing realities of our universe could be so intricate and complex that even today we have unanswered questions, and to have faith that it all occurred without intelligent design.

After all, with all of man's intelligence over the centuries, we still lack answers. Did it happen by itself, or does the intricate design imply an intelligent creative designer?

The idea that the complex world in which we live requires the intelligence of a designer, God, is a simple concept to grasp but the ramifications quickly become very complex.

Historically many statements from Scripture which were laughed at by some of the brightest scientific minds of their eras have since been proved to be correct. Similarly, valid aspects of science have been ridiculed by well meaning "believers." God light, whether natural physical light or spiritual light, is simultaneously wonderfully simple and profoundly complex.

The evidence that unseen physical light is all around us is undeniable. Light makes visible our surroundings. At the same time, we must acknowledge that we seldom give much thought to the abundant evidence of the presence of physical light.

The same is true with regard to spiritual light. The evidence of a Creator-Author of life is all around us. God has told us in His Word that creation itself is enough to confirm His existence (Romans 1:18-20).

God light, both in the form of physical light and spiritual light, is so abundant yet so often unappreciated by mankind.

Sunlight / Sonlight

Sunlight exists around us, yet we do not fully understand it or its essential role in all life.

Sonlight exists around us, yet we do not fully understand it or its essential role in all life.

THINK AND GROW

1. What evidences can you list of a Creator-Author of Life?

2. God designed, created, and maintains everything! Can you trust the details of your life to Him?

3. The message of salvation through Jesus Christ is complex and yet very simple. Can you explain it very simply?

22

Earth Light

There is a story told of some classroom experiments that happened many years ago. Each term a physics instructor would leave the laboratory for an entire class period with simple instructions: "I will be back at the end of the class period to pick up a list from each of you. You are to list everything that is in this laboratory. You are to work independently. Your goal is to develop as complete a list as possible."

At the professor's retirement, he was asked why he had maintained this habit year after year throughout his long career. "Why, I was testing for how observant students are," was the professor's response. "I never once received a complete list."

"But surely at least one of your students provided with you a complete list," came the retort. "No," replied the very distinguished professor. "In fact, in all my years no one ever listed light as being in the laboratory!"

It is hard for us to imagine many things which are more universal than light, or which are so taken for granted. Just as those students, we normally give little thought to light.

The final parallel is clearly before us. Sonlight is taken for granted and unappreciated regarding His role as Creator and as the sustainer of life. The Light of the world while on earth was not widely appreciated. His teachings conflicted with the religious leaders of the day and as a result He suffered much. And today the Spirit of God and the children of light are little noticed as they operate silently out of the limelight.

It is the author's sincere desire that the Beloved Apostle's statement might be true for you. "And these things we write to you that your joy may be full. This is the message which we have heard from Him and declare to you, that God is light and in Him there is no darkness at all" (1 John 1:4-5).

May your joy be full and complete as you more fully contemplate the God who is light.

Sunlight / Sonlight

Sunlight and all its benefits to us are often not appreciated.

Sonlight and His work on our behalf are often not appreciated.

THINK AND GROW

1. Make a list of other items which humans typically take for granted.

2. Why do you think we have a tendency to take vitally important things for granted, not thinking about the consequences of not having them?

Bonus Material:
THE BIG PICTURE

~ Overview of Light in Scripture ~

Forgive me for being so ordinary

while claiming to know

so extraordinary a God.

Jim Elliot

So, we are lying if we say

we have fellowship with God

but go on living in spiritual darkness;

we are not practicing the truth.

1 John 1:6

23

The Light of The World

The Bible is primarily the progressive revelation of Jesus Christ. The very Son of God is seen by the serious Bible scholar in the opening sentence of Scripture: "In the beginning God created the heavens and the earth" (Genesis 1:1). It is commonly understood that the word used for God in the original language, the word Elohim, is a uni-plural noun which shows the work of the triune God in creation. Throughout the entire Old Testament Christ is clearly seen. Some excellent books have been written which help the inquiring student to see Jesus Christ throughout the Old Testament. In Malachi, chapter 4, the last chapter of the Old Testament, we see Jesus Christ referred to as the "Sun of Righteousness" (Malachi 4:2).

The New Testament continues to reveal the Lord Jesus Christ to the serious Bible student. It opens with four separate parallel accounts of Jesus Christ's physical life on earth. One of those accounts, John's, opens with a reference to creation: "In the beginning was the Word [Jesus Christ], and the Word [Jesus Christ] was with God, and the Word [Jesus Christ] was God. He was in the beginning with God. All things were made through Him, and without Him nothing was made that was made" (John 1:1-3).

John then quickly brings us to the subject of light and the life that it produces. We read: "In Him was life, and that life was the light of men" (John 1:4). Notice that this verse does not say life was created, but rather life existed in Jesus Christ. Mankind, and everything else, is dependent upon God for life. God's power is necessary for both physical and spiritual life. Jesus Christ is eternal without need of any external sustaining power. Sunlight is necessary for physical life. Sonlight is necessary for spiritual life. Throughout his gospel John continues this theme of Jesus Christ being both light and life (examples include 5:26, 6:57, 8:12, 10:10, 11:25, 14:6, 17:3, 20:31).

The Gospel of John makes it clear that Jesus Christ is the true light (John 1:9). Later John records the Lord Jesus' words: "*I am* the light of the world" (John 8:12, emphasis added). This is one of the great "I AM's" of the Scriptures. It is the second of eight "I am" claims of our Lord recorded by John in his gospel.

The Creator gave us sunlight at the time of creation. Later the Son of God came to earth to more fully reveal God to mankind. He entered our world to bring light and spiritual life (Isaiah 9:2). Jesus Christ is both light and life. Individuals who understand and appropriate the spiritual life which comes from Him become children of light (John 12:35-36). The Word of God first mentions physical light at creation and tells us that when individuals receive spiritual light, they are part of the new creation (2 Corinthians 4:3-6, 5:17).

Finally, in Revelation we see the consummation of all things. In the last chapter we read regarding heaven: "There shall be no night there: They need no lamp nor light of the sun, for the Lord God gives them light" (Revelation 22:5). The sun represents daytime, and the lamp is indicative of night. Notice that man makes the lamp, but the sun was a creation of God. Neither lights at night nor the light of the sun during the day will be required in heaven. Everything that is needed and suits our needs on this planet will be past. Day and night are man's most basic means of marking time. In heaven time will be no more. Finally, in the last two verses of Revelation we find the last promise and the last prayer of the Bible, and our Lord Jesus is preeminent, as we read: "He who testifies to these things says, 'Surely I am coming quickly.' Amen. Even so, come, Lord Jesus! The grace of our Lord Jesus Christ *be* with you all. Amen."

The Bible is the progressive revelation of Jesus Christ, The Light of the World.

~ *Quote* ~ Jesus Christ Is The True Light: "For those of you who have discovered many of these areas this afternoon. Just a few. Let me suggest a reason and an explanation you may never have heard regarding a couple of things that John says about the Lord Jesus. In chapter 1, [1 John] we find Him called the true Light. Chapter 1 says, 'That was the True Light which lights every man, coming into the world' [John 1:9].

If the Lord Jesus has created nature, and we have the right and the responsibility to find Him in nature, then this thing we see about us that we call light, that whereby we perceive color, that whereby we see at all, that whereby things grow, light. Scripture says Jesus was the true light. Meaning what? Not that light which we see is false. Not that the light which we see is something that isn't real. And yet, I like Moffatt's translation of that which says that He was the real light. He was the real light. Moffatt consistently throughout his translation of John's Gospel translates the word truth as reality and the word true as real. And it's interesting to me that *the Scriptures show us that light as we see it, and as we enjoy its benefits is only not a false light, but a representation of the real light.*" —Jim Elliot (The Feeding of the Multitudes)

Sunlight / Sonlight

Sunlight is the source of physical life on earth.

Sonlight is the source of spiritual life on earth.

THINK AND GROW

Key Concept: The theme of the entire Bible, from Genesis 1 through Revelation 22, is Jesus Christ—the Son of God.

24

Creation

The Bible gives us one short sentence with respect to the creation of the cosmos. "In the beginning God created the heavens and the earth" (Genesis 1:1). And John opens his gospel by referencing that Jesus Christ was not only there "in the beginning" but was a part of the creative act.

There are five things which science has relentlessly studied. Each of the five is knowable to a degree. The five are: *time, force, action, space,* and *matter.* God has given us information about all five in the ten words of the very first verse of the Bible. "In the beginning God created the heavens and the earth" (Genesis 1:1).

First: *Time.* "In the *beginning...*" The Word of God tells us that God is an eternal being—He has an eternal past and an eternal future. In these first three words of Scripture we find that time begins. "All honor and glory to God forever and ever! He is the eternal King, the unseen One who never dies; He alone is God" (1 Timothy 1:17).

Second: *Force.* "In the beginning *God...*" The Bible tells us that God is omnipotent, or all-powerful. God's power is without limit. "For by Him all things were created that are in heaven and that are on earth, visible and invisible, whether thrones or dominions or principalities or powers. All things were created through Him and for Him. And He is before all things, and in Him all things consist" (Colossians 1:16-17).

Third: *Action.* "In the beginning God *created...*" The Scripture tells us that mankind was created "in the image of God" (Genesis 1:27). Man, as he was created reflected his creative Maker. Sin entered and man died spiritually. Today those who have accepted God's plan of salvation are becoming increasingly like God. "But we all, with unveiled face, beholding as in a mirror the glory of the Lord, are being transformed into the same image from glory to glory, just as by the Spirit of the Lord" (2 Corinthians 3:18).

Fourth: *Space.* "In the beginning God created *the heavens...*" Every day astronomers are discovering greater magnitudes of glory in space than ever imagined. The Word of God tells us that "the heavens declare the glory of God" (Psalm 19:1a).

Fifth: *Matter.* "In the beginning God created the heavens and *the earth.*" God created the earth with all its beauty for mankind. Even today scientists and researchers in many fields are daily discovering greater depths of intricacy of design on this marvelous planet we call earth. "The earth displays His handiwork" (Psalm 19:1b).

"In the beginning [time] God [force] created [action] the heavens [space] and the earth [matter]" (Genesis 1:1).

Genesis 1:1 introduces us to five profound concepts with just ten words.

An old battle continues to be debated. On one side are those who on faith are willing to believe that God is great enough to have done exactly what He said, and it doesn't really matter if it fits our human conceptions and understandings. On the other side are those who on faith believe that the evolutionary process accounts for all of the grandeur and beauty of this existence that we call life. On the side of the creationists there should be the willingness to say, "We don't fully understand it all, and that's not surprising, because if we did, we would be equal with God. However, based upon the proven reality of God in other ways, we accept God at His Word."

On the other hand the evolutionists should be willing to say, "We know we don't have scientific evidence for all that we postulate, but we have faith that our postulates are correct, and some day we will be able to prove them beyond any reasonable doubt."

In the first case you need a clear view of God in order to have the faith required to find creationism an acceptable and comfortable alternative. In the second case you must have some doubt regarding the accuracy of the Word of God, and you must have faith in a group of unproven postulates.

The unfortunate thing in this regard is that many well-meaning creationists try to make the first chapter of Genesis say more than it does. Many emotional and credibility-lacking arguments hurt the true creationist's position rather than help it. It is no comfort to note that the same can be said about many arguments emanating from those who hold to unproven postulates.

The question revolves largely around your view of God. How big is your God? Someone once remarked regarding the story of Jonah, "I believe Jonah could have swallowed the great fish whole if God had so chosen." Is that irresponsible faith? Or is that a belief in a big God? How big is your God?

In the first recorded words of God we read, "And God said, let there be light: and there was light" (Genesis 1:3). Notice also that during the first day of creation there was a dividing of light from darkness. "God saw that the light was good, and He separated the light from the darkness" (Genesis 1:4).

God is light. Jesus Christ is God. Jesus Christ causes division.

We read in the gospel of John: "And this is the condemnation, that the light has come into the world, and men loved darkness rather than light, because their deeds were evil. For everyone practicing evil hates the light and does not come to the light, lest his deeds should be exposed. But he who does the truth comes to the light, that his deeds may be clearly seen, that they have been done in God" (John 3:19-21). The reality of God causes a separation. We see a parallel in the animal world where some creatures come out as the sun rises; others hide until the darkness comes, at which time they come forth. At sunrise the world becomes a cheerful place as the birds and animals of the day awaken with song. The same rising sun causes bats, owls, and some beasts to seek the cover of darkness. The presence of light awakens and attracts some but repels others.

Jesus Christ is the great spiritual sunrise. "The rising Sun will come to us from heaven to shine on those living in darkness" (Luke 1:78-79 niv). And the Apostle Peter wrote: "You'll do well to keep focusing on it. It's the one light you have in a dark time as you wait for daybreak and the rising of the Morning Star in your hearts" (2 Peter 1:19 The Message). In the original language the word "morning star" used here means the "light bringer." In Revelation chapters 2 and 22 we find Jesus Christ referred to as "the Morning Star." Christ Himself is the Morning Star. The reference is to the arising of Christ in our hearts. As children of light we are to be looking for Him, His second coming, with eager expectation. Jesus Christ is the great Sonrise, and as children of light we are awaiting the dawn of His return.

In the creation account in Genesis there is a parallelism between the first set of three days and the second set of three days. In day one light and darkness were separated; and then in day four the sun, moon, and stars were made visible. In day two land and water were separated; and then in day five animals were created in various forms for land and sea. Note too that the word "created" here is the same word as was used in Genesis 1:1. On the third day vegetation came forth; and then on day six God "created" man. Vegetation is the source of man's energy and sustenance whether he eats vegetation directly or after it has been consumed by animal life. The seventh day, we read, was God's day of rest.

The fourth day has some very interesting aspects for us to consider. We read: "And God said, 'Let there be lights in the expanse of the sky to separate the day from the night, and let them serve as signs to mark the seasons and days and years, and let them be lights in the expanse of the sky to give light on the earth.' And it was so. God made two great lights—the greater light to govern the day and the lesser light to govern the night. He also made the stars. God set them in the expanse of the sky to give light on the earth, to govern the day and the night, and to separate light from darkness. And God saw that it was good. And there was evening, and there was morning—the fourth day" (Genesis 1:14-19 niv).

Note in verse fourteen that the reason given for making visible the sun, moon, and stars was twofold. First, "let them serve as signs," and second, "and to mark the seasons and days and years."

Living in our enlightened day few people would question the second reason given. We know the role of the sun and moon with respect to days, seasons, and years. Day and night on earth are determined by one rotation of the planet. The side of the earth facing the sun is in sunlight or daytime. Our seasons are the result of the relationship of the orbits of the celestial bodies, and our planet's years are governed by its orbit around the sun once every year.

Another reason we are given for the making visible of the sun, moon, and stars has to do with being "signs."

The greater light referred to is our sun. This greater light we have considered earlier to some extent as we considered the nature of light. All of our natural light comes to us from the sun.

Jesus Christ, and the redemption and salvation that He provides, is the theme of the Bible from beginning to end. In the Old Testament we have to look a little harder to see Christ, but He is there.

The greater light, our physical sun, is a type or foreshadowing of "the Sun of Righteousness," our Lord Jesus Christ, of Malachi 4:2. The physical sun which gives light and life to the earth is a sign of the Son of God. When Jesus Christ came to earth, it was what might be considered the midday of human history. The earth was under the full blaze of the Son of righteousness' spiritual light, and just as the physical sun produces differing reactions in different substances, so too the Son of God's blazing righteousness caused a separation with respect to man's reaction to that life and light.

In Genesis 1:3 God caused a separation in light and darkness, but it wasn't until some time later in Genesis 1:16 that God made the sun and moon visible to the earth. In the time between verse 3 and verse 16 the sun was there and was giving forth light, but it was not seen.

Our world today is in a similar state. Jesus Christ, the Light of the world and the Sun of righteousness, is giving spiritual light, but He is not seen by the world at large. The greater light, our sun, is a foreshadowing or a type of the Sun of righteousness, Jesus Christ.

Notice that in Genesis 1:16 a lesser light is also mentioned. This is clearly our moon. What are some of the more important characteristics of our moon? First, notice that the moon is a dead body; it has neither life nor light. The moon reflects the light of the sun. Second, notice that we have full moons, half moons, quarter moons, and so forth. That is, the moon must be in proper relationship to the sun if it is to reflect the sun's light to earth.

We find that the lesser light, our moon, is a picture, type, or foreshadowing of the true Church. Christ's desire is that His Church will reflect His light to a dark and needy world. It is only when the Church is in proper relationship to Christ that it can reflect the love and light and life of Christ to this earth. This Church has no light of its own but must reflect the Sun of righteousness by being in proper relationship.

Jesus Christ came to earth and dwelt among men, but today He is beyond the horizon and there can be no direct viewing of Him. If the world is to see Jesus Christ, it must be as the Church, acting as the lesser light, reflects His radiance and beauty to this earth. We read in Matthew: "Let your light so shine before men, that they may see your good works and glorify your Father in heaven" (Matthew 5:16).

The sun and moon were made visible as signs. They are signs, foreshadows, of Jesus Christ, the Sun of righteousness, and of His Church, which reflects the only true light.

One might wonder about the stars referred to in this portion of Genesis chapter one. Some believe that the stars are individual Christians; however, I believe that the stars primarily represent the Jewish people and secondarily all members of His church. Stars are interesting in several ways. First of all, stars are sources of light. Second, stars are scattered across our sky, or more correctly, throughout the cosmos. Finally, stars are standards for navigation and for the telling of time.

The stars are a sign of Israel. The nation Israel is God's chosen people and has existed to give mankind spiritual light. In fact, it was the nation of Israel that provided us with the Scriptures. Secondly, notice that the Jewish people have been scattered across the entire face of the earth in a way unparalleled by any other nation. Additionally, as students of prophecy know, Israel is God's key to understanding the plan of redemption and to the understanding of the times and of God's clock.

In the Scriptures we read about the Abrahamic covenant:

"I will surely bless you and make your descendants as numerous as the stars in the sky" (Genesis 22:17 niv), and "the Lord had promised to make Israel as numerous as the stars in the sky" (1 Chronicles 27:23 niv). In the great spiritual hall of fame in our New Testament we read concerning Abraham, "And so from this one man ... came descendants as numerous as the stars in the sky" (Hebrews 11:12 niv).

Jesus Christ, the true light, came to this world from within the Jewish nation. A prophecy in the Book of Numbers, "a Star shall come out of Jacob" (Numbers 24:17), was fulfilled by Jesus Christ. At His coming the "star in the east" (Matthew 2:2) over Bethlehem symbolically announced the coming of the true light.

The creation account in the Bible presents Jesus Christ, who is the true light, as "the greater light." The greater light, our sun as we have previously seen, is the source of all light and life on this habitation we call earth. The greater light is truly the physical light of the world. Jesus Christ is just as truly the spiritual light of the world. In the creation account both the physical light of the world and the spiritual light of the world are clearly seen. The lesser light, the moon, today is a picture of the true Church of Jesus Christ. The Church is to reflect the Sonlight to this earth "because in this world we are like Him" (1 John 4:17 niv).

The Jewish people are sources of light, they are scattered, and they provide the keys to understanding the Scriptures and the telling of prophetic time.

Sunlight / Sonlight

Sunlight causes a division between light and darkness, and day and night.

Sonlight causes a division between true and false, and good and evil.

THINK AND GROW

1. What do the greater light, lesser light, and stars in creation (Genesis 1:14-19) represent from a spiritual viewpoint?

2. Write a paragraph for each (greater light, lesser light, stars) that would explain them to a junior high student.

25

Greater Light

In the ninth chapter of the gospel of John an event in the life of Jesus is recorded. "Now as Jesus passed by, He saw a man who was blind from birth" (verse 1). "'As long as I am in the world, I am the light of the world.' When He had said these things, He spat on the ground and made clay with the saliva; and He anointed the eyes of the blind man with the clay. And He said to him, 'Go, wash in the pool of Siloam' (which is translated, Sent). So, he went and washed, and came back seeing" (verses 5-7). The chapter continues the story, including the disbelief of some that this could be the same one who had previously "sat and begged."

The human tragedy of blindness in that day would be hard to overstate. Envision a typical blind person of that day seated by the roadside. A man of but 35 would appear twice his age. His clothes would be dirty and ragged, and the odor about him repugnant to those accustomed to daily bathing.

He may have had a bright mind as a youth but was never understood by those who were to mold his future. All because he was different from most people; he was totally blind from birth. And not only was he blind, but his face was disfigured where his eyes should have been. As a youth he was ridiculed. As an adult he was still an outcast.

Think if you will beyond the human tragedy this represents and reflect upon the reality of what it means to be blind. As an infant he had never known the loving looks of his parents as they cradled him in their arms. As a young boy he had never seen a butterfly nor a flower nor a tree. He was never able to participate in most of the games other children played. He had never seen a book or a school.

As a young man he was often the object of cruel jokes. Occasionally young bullies would have great sport in verbally and physically taunting and abusing him. He didn't even have the satisfaction of seeing his tormentors.

Color is an abstract concept to this man. What does it mean to say green grass, yellow lights, or a blue ocean? He can only imagine, but even imagination is difficult since he has never seen anything. He is totally blind and has been that way since birth.

Unfortunately, this man's life goes on with no hope for change. But imagine for a minute that you are this man and that from some miraculous process you suddenly one day gain sight for the first time. What would your reaction be?

Notice that the blind man of John's gospel had to have enough faith in Christ to do as he was told. He had to believe Christ enough to go and wash in the particular spot he was told. What he was told to do seemed foolish to the crowd. After all, spit and dirt mixed to form mud and then put on the eyes of one who had been blind from birth—really now! But the physically blind man had faith in Jesus Christ and received his physical sight because of Christ's work and his own faith.

The Scriptures have a lot to say about blindness, and many times physical blindness is used to describe spiritual blindness. We will go back to the Old Testament to pick up some thoughts concerning Jesus Christ, the greater light, before we explore this subject further.

Israel is God's chosen people. The account of God's dealings with the Jewish people is given primarily in the Old Testament. But throughout the Old Testament the great plan of redemption is forecast through types and foreshadowings. It is commonly reported that there are hundreds of prophecies concerning Jesus Christ in the Old Testament.

For instance, the Cross of Calvary is seen clearly in Psalm 22, Isaiah 53, and other passages.

Our interest is with respect to Jesus Christ as the light of the world. We will look primarily at the writings of the prophet Isaiah since he provides a remarkably clear portrayal of the coming Messiah, Jesus Christ. The Book of Isaiah has been described as a miniature Bible. The subject of Isaiah is Christ, just as the subject of the Bible is Christ. The book of Isaiah is divided into 66 chapters, which are further divided into two parts of 39 and 27 chapters each. These two portions correspond to the 39 books of the Old Testament and the 27 books of the New Testament. The book may also be thought of as "the gospel according to Isaiah," with the key word being salvation. The first 39 chapters deal with God's holiness, and we see mankind failing to live up to the requirements of an absolutely righteous God. In chapter 42 Isaiah presents another vision of the coming Messiah; we read: "I the Lord, have called You in righteousness, and will hold Your hand; I will keep You and give You as a covenant to the people, as *a light to the Gentiles, to open blind eyes*" (Isaiah 42:6-7, emphasis added). And in Isaiah 49:6 we find, "I will also give You as *a light to the Gentiles*, that You should be My salvation to the ends of the earth" (emphasis added).

Presented in these verses are prophecies concerning the coming Messiah, Jesus Christ. Coming out of the nation Israel, He will be the light of the world and He will bring salvation to the Gentiles. Since the Cross of Calvary, Jesus Christ has been forming His Church, made up of believing Jews and believing Gentiles in this present period of time.

These prophecies concerning the Messiah have been fulfilled. Consider the words of Simeon (who Scripture says in Luke 2:25 was "just and devout, waiting for the consolation of Israel") recorded in Luke chapter two: "Sovereign Lord, as You have promised, You now dismiss your servant in peace. For my eyes have seen Your salvation, which You have prepared in the sight of all the people, a light for revelation to the Gentiles and for glory to Your people Israel" (Luke 2:29-32 niv). A similar reference is made in Acts 26:23, showing that these prophecies of Isaiah were fulfilled in Jesus Christ.

As we now consider the New Testament, we will look primarily at the gospel of John.

In the early portion of John chapter one we find John the Baptist bearing witness of the true Light. John was "not that Light" but was bearing witness of the true Light. We read: "There was a man sent from God, whose name was John. This man came for a witness, to bear witness of the Light, that all through him might believe. He was not that Light but was sent to bear witness of that Light" (John 1:6-8). Notice that John is using the word Light as a proper noun, as a name for Jesus Christ. God is light. Jesus Christ is God. Therefore, Jesus Christ is light. Jesus Christ came to earth in human form and was the light of the world. John then continues as he speaks of Jesus Christ: "That was the true Light which gives light to every man coming into the world. He was in the world, and the world was made through Him, and the world did not know Him. He came to His own, and His own did not receive Him" (John 1:9-11).

In broad strokes the apostle John first reminds us that Jesus Christ was involved in the creation of the universe. That is, Jesus Christ is truly part of the eternal Godhead, both eternity past and eternity future. John then reminds us that Christ was rejected by His own people, that is the Jewish nation. Even prior to these words, in the opening five verses of his gospel, John has forcefully told us that Jesus Christ was in the beginning.

During our Lord's ministry, He referred to Himself directly as the light of the world. For instance, "Then Jesus spoke to them again, saying, 'I am the light of the world. He who follows Me shall not walk in darkness but have the light of life'" (John 8:12). And again, we read in the next chapter, "As long as I am in the world, I am the light of the world" (John 9:5).

Jesus Christ is the spiritual light of the world. God is light. Jesus Christ claimed to be the very Son of God. How you react to the claims of Jesus Christ determines whether you are walking in the radiance of His Sonshine or are a creature of the night. As we have seen, Jesus Christ knew that He would be divisive, that some would accept Him as the true light and others would not. Listen to His own words: "Are there not twelve hours of daylight? A man who walks by day will not stumble, for he sees by this world's light. It is when he walks by night that he stumbles, for he has no light" (John 11:9-10 niv).

Repeatedly Jesus Christ claimed to be one with the Father, that He was God. Jesus Christ came to earth as a man, even though He was fully and truly God. Speaking of the Father, Jesus said, "When a man believes in Me, he does not believe in Me only, but in the One who sent Me. When he looks at Me, he sees the one who sent Me. I have come into the world as a light, so that no one who believes in Me should stay in darkness" (John 12:44-46).

Jesus Christ came to earth to remove the penalty of sin from those who are willing to trust Him, the very creator of the world. Sin is often equated with darkness in Scripture.

Plato wrote, "We can easily forgive a child who is afraid of the dark; the real tragedy of life is when men are afraid of the light."

Throughout Scripture we see the concept of spiritual blindness. It is this form of blindness that keeps some people from accepting Jesus Christ as their Savior. They may be blind, but they do not realize it. Just as the physically blind man cannot comprehend sight except as an abstract idea, so too the spiritually blind cannot comprehend spiritual sight. The god of this world (Satan) has blinded them with spiritual blindness. We read in 2 Corinthians 4:4 (niv), "The god of this age has blinded the minds of unbelievers, so that they cannot see the light of the gospel of the glory of Christ, Who is the image of God." And then we see the contrast of those who have gained spiritual sight in verse 6: "For it is the God who commanded light to shine out of darkness, who has shone in our hearts to give the light of the knowledge of the glory of God in the face of Jesus Christ."

This is the very core of the message of the Bible, that man, since the fall in the Garden of Eden, is spiritually blind. Man, since that time has a sin nature. Jesus Christ offers the only true way to spiritual sight and wholeness. Jesus Christ is truth. Jesus Christ is the only source of true life. "I [Jesus Christ] am the way and the truth and the life" (John 14:6). Just as the sun provides physical life on this earth, the Son provides spiritual life. "I [Jesus Christ] have come that they may have life, and that they may have it more abundantly" (John 10:10 niv explanation added).

There is a parallel between the formless void of creation in Genesis 1:1-2 and the emptiness that exists deep within man without Jesus Christ. The heart is an empty, formless void looking for fulfillment until Christ enters in.

Peter Ilich Tchaikovsky, a great genius of music, summed up mankind's dilemma when he wrote, "The greater reason I have to be happy, the more discontented I become." The only way to find peace, satisfaction, meaning, and order in life is by allowing the Creator access to your heart. When the rays of the Son are allowed to burst forth into the heart, darkness and gloom are dispelled.

Jesus Christ is truth. Jesus Christ is the only answer for spiritual blindness. Spiritual life is gained in the same way that physical life is obtained, that is through birth. "You should not be surprised by My saying, 'You must be born again'" (John 3:7 niv). This spiritual life is eternal rather than mortal as physical life. "For you have been born again, not of perishable seed, but of imperishable, through the living and enduring Word of God" (1 Peter 1:23 niv). Jesus Christ is the only way to obtain eternal spiritual life.

Spiritual life is only possible for us because of the Cross. God is a holy, righteous God. God cannot look upon or tolerate sin. Sin separates man from God. Separation from God is spiritual death, the opposite of spiritual life, which is uniting with God. It is not a coincidence that when Jesus Christ bore our sin on the Cross of Calvary, darkness covered the land, "Now from the sixth hour until the ninth hour there was darkness over all the land" (Matthew 27:45). God is light. Jesus Christ is God. When Jesus bore our sins, He was separated by our sin from the Father. "My God, My God, why have You forsaken Me?" (Matthew 27:46.) Sin is so terrible that even when the very Son of God took our sin upon Him, it caused a separation from the Father. At midday from noon until 3:00 p.m. darkness covered the land.

The biblical account does not end at Calvary; Jesus Christ rose from the dead. He conquered both physical death and spiritual death. We read that "His appearance was like lightning, and His clothes were white as snow" (Matthew 28:3 niv). God is light. Jesus Christ rose from the grave with His countenance like lightning.

One may intellectually assimilate the meaning of the Cross without realizing a personal need for Christ's dying for the sins of the world.

Years ago, a bank robber was apprehended in our city as he was leaving the scene of the crime, money in hand. He insisted that he was not a thief. When his case came to trial, he insisted that he was not a thief and that this was his first time at robbery. He was found guilty. How many robberies does someone have to commit to be considered a thief?

I read once of a patient in a hospital who refused to believe she was sick. She had been assured by her physicians that her illness was terminal, yet she refused to believe she was sick. Her mind dwelt upon the fact that she had good muscle tone, that her heart and cardiopulmonary system were good. She had no broken bones and didn't even have a cold or the flu. She died insisting she was healthy. How many diseases must someone have to be considered sick?

How many sins does a person need to commit to be a sinner?

There are two kinds of blindness corresponding to two kinds of sight. As you read, you are utilizing your physical sight. It is possible, however, to read without spiritual sight. If you have spiritual sight, you know it as surely as you know that you have physical sight. If as you read these words you recognize your need of spiritual sight, you can gain it by simply asking Jesus Christ, the light of the world, to enter into your heart and give you spiritual sight. Christ promises to do so, but only on a conditional basis. The conditions are these: First, you must acknowledge that you have sinned. Second, you must want to turn away from your sin and desire to live a righteous life. Third, you must believe that Jesus is the very Son of God as He claims to be, and that He died for you. If you turn to Christ in prayer the best you know how, He will enter into your life and give you spiritual sight. You will be able to affirm as did the physically blind man of John 9:25 (niv): "One thing I do know. I was blind but now I see!" If you have not received spiritual sight, you are worse off than the blind man described at the beginning of this chapter. If you have received spiritual sight, you know the reality of spiritual things as surely as the person who has gained physical sight knows the reality of material things.

Just as the sun is the greater light in our physical world, the Son is the true light—the greater light in the spiritual world.

Sunlight / Sonlight

Sunlight allows humans to have physical sight.

Sonlight allows humans to have spiritual sight.

THINK AND GROW

1. Have you known a child who was very afraid of the dark?

2. Have you known an adult who seemed unwilling to consider the truths of the Bible?

3. In what ways are they similar? Different?

26

Lesser Light

My boyhood home from the time I was eight years old was an interesting place. The house in which we lived was unusual in several ways. It had been built in 1909 and completely remodeled in 1911. The house was positioned on a large city lot in such a way that it had a huge front yard with lots of fruit trees and virtually no back yard.

To me the best thing was its location. The house sat on a three-way corner that was very much the shape of a Y. At the time we moved into the house, the lot across the street was occupied by the basement remains of a laundry facility that had burned to the ground. It was a great place for a young boy to play and to get into trouble. It wasn't long, however, before a four-plex was built on that spot.

The third corner lot belonged to "old Mr. Stuart" as I affectionately called him. He was a widower who lived there together with his sister in their sunset years.

Mr. Stuart's yard was always immaculate, and his small house was always maintained in a trim manner that seemed inappropriate for this aging part of town. But best of all, old Mr. Stuart was my personal friend. I remember the times when Mr. Stuart would help my newly acquired stepfather (my father had died when I was an infant) with pouring concrete, repairing plumbing, or some other job that needed doing. Mr. Stuart had a way of acknowledging me and making me feel important. Sometimes it would just be a smile as his eyes caught me intensely watching him laboring. Other times it would be the way he brought me into the conversation during breaks. Sometimes Mr. Stuart would even ask my advice. There was something special between us that did not exist between Mr. Stuart and my older brother or sister or with any of the other kids in the neighborhood. He was a special kind of man that a young boy could admire. His favorite sandwich was peanut butter and onions.

One of my most vivid memories of Mr. Stuart revolves around the first of many trips I took to his workshop. I had acquired an old bicycle from my grandfather in Canada, and it was the first possession of my very own that I really cared about. It was old, but it was mine. One day a nut had fallen off the bolt that attached the front fender to the bicycle fork. I did not notice it until the bolt had worked its way out and the fender was free to sag and cause all kinds of terrifying noises as it interfered with the front wheel and the fork.

At the time this occurred, I was only two blocks from home, but the slow careful walk home seemed like twenty miles as I contemplated the ruined bicycle that I loved so much. As I approached my home, old Mr. Stuart was out pushing his lawn mower over his carpet-like lawn. I figured that he must really enjoy mowing the lawn. He saw a tear in my eye as I pushed that bicycle with one hand on the handlebar and the other hand, in a comforting fashion, holding the front fender up into its proper position. Mr. Stuart immediately came to me and put his arm around me, and his loving voice said, "Let's work on that together. I just might have what we need to fix it!"

His little house wasn't much bigger than a double-car garage, but after entering the door into the kitchen, he turned and opened what looked like a closet door and we started down some narrow stairs. He explained that he kept his tools in the basement. Prior to this I had no idea his little white house had a basement.

The stairwell was very dark. There was a single light bulb in the center of the basement that shed a small amount of light on the stairs. Since my eyes were not dark-adapted after coming in from the bright sunshine and since Mr. Stuart's big broad frame cast a large shadow, I had to feel for each step with my feet.

Arriving in the basement, I could see that the central portion contained a large old furnace and fuel bin that took up about one-quarter of the space. The rest of the room was covered with cobwebs. But in one corner was a small room, probably about four feet by twelve feet. The door in the narrow end allowed passage into the workshop. Inside his work area it was dark. The first thing old Mr. Stuart did was to light up one of his pipes, filling the room with a new odor masking the musty smell, but nearly gagging me. I could see very little.

On the long side towards the outside of the house was a workbench the full length of the room. In the center was a small window about one foot by two feet, which was below ground level and had a window well around it to keep the dirt back. The combination of shrubbery, the window well, and years of accumulated dirt on both sides of the glass made this a window in name only. Little or no light came through. There was one small light bulb, probably about a 25-watt, which in contrast to the bare bulb in the main portion of the basement had a shield extending out over the top of it and slanting downward to its edges. The underside of this shield had originally been white in order to serve as a reflector, but by now it had aged to a medium brown color. It was still among the lightest colored objects in the room.

Other than a small area about three feet wide by 18 to 24 inches deep on the workbench below the window, the entire room including the rafters above was packed with tools and supplies. It seemed like hundreds of jars and cans, none of which was labeled, filled the shelves, nooks, and corners. But as I would learn through the years, old Mr. Stuart knew every item that he had, where it was, and how he had obtained it.

Mr. Stuart tilted the shield of the light to provide light higher into a corner behind him and then reached high and pulled out a large can that he then turned over on the open spot on the workbench. His large tough-skinned, multi-scarred fingers spread the pile of screws and bolts evenly. Suddenly he reached for a used bolt and said, "That's the one you need. I found it about three years ago near 34th and Belmont." He pushed the remaining pile off the workbench edge into the waiting coffee can, refilling this particular cache. Similarly, he retrieved a nut and then a lock washer. It wasn't but a few more minutes and my bicycle was fixed.

Over the years since I last saw Mr. Stuart I have often thought about his gracious nature and about his workshop.

Jesus Christ, the Master Craftsman, has His workshop on earth today. It is His Church composed of all true believers. He knows by name each individual believer, He knows just when they entered into His fold, and He knows just exactly what their strengths and weaknesses are. He also has a specific plan for each and every one. In regard to our heavenly Father's intimate knowledge of us we read: "Are not two sparrows sold for a penny? Yet not one of them will fall to the ground apart from the will of your Father. And even the very hairs of your head are all numbered. So, don't be afraid; you are worth more value than many sparrows" (Matthew 10:29-31 niv).

There are two ways of seeing God light; one can see either the source or a reflection of the source. Jesus Christ is the source. His church, and the individuals who make up His true church are to reflect Him to their surroundings.

The true children of light have been given access to His nature (2 Peter 1:4). Unfortunately, their light is often dimmed because it is "hidden under a bushel" (Matthew 5:15-16), a picture of our inability and unwillingness to walk in our new nature. Another key reason our light is often obscured and unrecognized is the spiritual blindness of those around us (Matthew 15:12-14).

These sad realities bring us back to the great contrast between God light and children of light. God light is eternally unchanging and absolutely dependable. Children of light while still on earth are fickle and inconsistent. In the future New Creation children of light will be like Him!

Today the Church is the lesser light of Genesis 1:16. The fact is that Jesus Christ is the true light, just as our sun is the true light of this planet. However, when the sun is not visible, we still receive light from the sun as it is reflected off the moon. The lesser light, the spiritual moon, today is the Church, whose role it is to reflect the light and beauty of Christ to a dark and needy world. Listen to the words of Jesus Christ: *As long as I am in the world,* I am the light of the world" (John 9:5, emphasis added). There is a hint here that while Jesus Christ was the light of the world while on earth, there may come a new light. Later we find references to believers as the light of the world, such as in Acts 13:47, "For so the Lord has commanded us [Paul and Barnabas]: *'I have set you as a light to the Gentiles, that you should be for salvation to the ends of the earth.'"*

"There is one glory of the sun, another glory of the moon, and another glory of the stars; for one star differs from another star in glory" (1 Corinthians 15:41). Jesus Christ clearly taught that individual Christians who make up the true Church are to be lights in this dark world. "You are the light of the world" (Matthew 5:14).

And in Paul's first letter to the Thessalonians we find: "But you, brethren, are not in darkness, so that this Day should overtake you as a thief. You are all sons of light and sons of the day. We are not of the night nor of darkness" (1 Thessalonians 5:4-5).

The Church, the lesser light, is clearly to be a light unto this dark world. The primary definition of the Church is all true believers in Jesus Christ from the time of Christ up through today and into the future up to the point that Christ returns to rapture the Church to be with Him as His bride forever and ever.

We have said earlier that Jesus Christ knows everything about us and that He has a plan for each one of us. The Word of God uses several metaphors to describe the true Church. One of these is that the Church is one body. In this case there are many members, but only one body. Christ is the head, you may be a wrist, and I may be an elbow, but all the members doing their appointed tasks make up one body. Some of the invisible members such as internal organs may be the most important. Some of the most visible members such as fingers or hands may be in reality less important. (A human body can adapt to the loss of a finger, hand, or even an arm, but can the human body adapt to the loss of its heart or liver?)

Unfortunately, the Evil One comes in and stirs up the pride in our Adamic nature so that many times members of the Church fight among themselves as each seeks to have the most prominent place. This is not God's plan.

As individual Christians we are to be lights in a dark and confused world. Where is light most needed? It does not require a lot of thought to realize that light is most needed where it is the darkest. John the Baptist was a light which showed the way during the darkness which preceded Christ's first coming. "He [John the Baptist] was the burning and shining lamp, and you were willing for a time to rejoice in his light" (John 5:35).

In Mr. Stuart's workshop the light was dependent upon one lone bulb to do its appointed task. We need to shine and light up the area around us wherever we are. The lone light bulb in a dark stairwell may very well be more important in God's eyes than any particular bulb among hundreds of other bulbs in a massive chandelier. Of how much consequence is a single burned-out bulb in a grand chandelier? How about a burned-out bulb in a stairwell? We need to be faithful where we are so that in the final day Philippians 2:15 (niv) may be true of us, "so that you may become blameless and pure, children of God without fault in a crooked and depraved generation, in which you shine like stars in the universe [some versions say lights in the world] as you hold out the word of life..." In the meantime, while we wait for that final day, may we be "giving thanks to the Father, who has qualified you to *share in the inheritance of the saints in the kingdom of light.* For He has *rescued us from the dominion of darkness,* and brought us into the kingdom of the Son He loves" (Colossians 1:12-13 niv, emphasis added).

As the lesser light, the moon, reflects the sunlight, the true Church is called upon to reflect Sonlight to a spiritually dark world. As we reflect His light, we must always remember that even the godliest person cannot create or generate light—the best we can do is reflect His light.

Sunlight / Sonlight

Even at night sunlight is often seen on earth as it is reflected off the surface of the moon.

Today while Sonlight has left earth "to prepare a place for His followers" (John 14:2), they are charged with reflecting His light to their surroundings.

THINK AND GROW

How would you characterize the relative importance of a single light in a dark place as compared to a single light which is part of a group of large bright chandeliers in a large ballroom?

27

New Creation

Have you ever considered how you could explain what earth is like to someone who had never seen the planet earth? It would be an extremely difficult, if not impossible, task. Likewise, there is no way for us to comprehend what heaven will be like.

The most concentrated description of heaven is given to us in the Book of Revelation, chapters 21 and 22, the last two chapters of our Bible. The predominant theme of these chapters is that everything is new. Heaven will be totally new, and there is no way we can grasp the magnificence, beauty, and joy of heaven.

We do have many other clues about heaven beyond what we find in Revelation. Both the Old and New Testaments have a lot to say about the coming new creation. The prophet Isaiah wrote, *"All the stars of the heavens will be dissolved* and the sky rolled up like a scroll; *all the starry host will fall* like withered leaves from the vine, like shriveled figs from the fig tree" (Isaiah 34:4 niv, emphasis added). "Lift up your eyes to the heavens, and look on the earth beneath. For *the heavens will vanish* away like smoke, the earth will grow old like a garment, and those who dwell in it will die in like manner; but My salvation will be forever, and My righteousness will not be abolished" (Isaiah 51:6 emphasis added). And the prophet Zechariah adds, "On that day there will be no light, no cold or frost. It will be a unique day, *without daytime or nighttime*—a day known to the Lord. When evening comes, *there will be light"* (Zechariah 14:6-7 niv, emphasis added).

One of the things we know about heaven is that time will be no more. It is not a question of endless time, but rather there will be no such thing as time. We will dwell in heaven as eternal beings, without aging or any other factors we associate with time.

The light of the new creation will be God Himself. Revelation 22:5 says, "There shall be no night there: They need no lamp nor light of the sun, for the Lord God gives them light. And they shall reign forever and ever."

Four obvious things stand out in these four phrases.

First, "There will be *no night* there." Night and darkness throughout Scripture represent evil, sin, and separation from God. God is light; where He is there can be no darkness. In 1 John 1:5 we read, "This is the message which we have heard from Him and declare to you, that God is light and in Him is no darkness at all." And Paul wrote in 2 Corinthians 6:14, "For what fellowship has righteousness with lawlessness? And what communion has light with darkness?" It is clear that where Jesus Christ is, there will be no darkness and no night. The first statement tells us there shall be no night. The separation of day and night is mankind's most basic form of discerning time. Time will be no more. We shall be with Him forever and ever.

Second, notice that there is *no need for lights or even the sun.* All we need here on earth will be passed. Even the sun which is essential for life on earth will be unnecessary in heaven. This second phrase is a beautiful expression which tells us all earthly cares and needs will be no more, we won't even have any need for external light.

Third, "*the Lord God gives them light.*" God is light. There will be no other lights, not even the sun, for God is the source of light.

Fourth, consider "*forever and ever.*" This is a reassuring statement of what has already been presented in the first three statements. We are partakers of the divine nature. The fourth phrase is like a summary, we shall be with Him forever and ever, eternal beings basking in the light, life, and love of God.

Another portion of John's description of heaven commands our attention: "And he carried me away in the Spirit to a mountain great and high, and showed me the Holy City, Jerusalem, coming down out of heaven from God. It shone with the glory of God, and its brilliance was like that of a very precious jewel, like a jasper, clear as crystal" (Revelation 21:10-11 niv). One thing we know is that the New Jerusalem will be filled with exquisite beauty.

Contemplate the most beautiful scene you have ever seen or imagined on earth. Think about that gorgeous grandeur of natural beauty. That scene will appear worse than any garbage dump compared to any aspect of the new heavenly Jerusalem. The new city will have the glory and dazzling radiance of God Himself. God is light! Light is what allows us to see the kaleidoscope we call color. Color is largely what provides beauty on earth. Jerusalem will be lit with the glory of God. In the New Jerusalem we will know what complete fulfillment and complete beauty are.

This new creation is not strictly a concept out of the Book of Revelation but is found throughout Scripture. For example, the prophet Isaiah wrote: "For behold, I create new heavens and a new earth; and the former shall not be remembered or come to mind. But be glad and rejoice forever in what I create; for behold, I create Jerusalem as a rejoicing, and her people a joy" (Isaiah 65:17-18). And we hear the words of the apostle Peter: "Nevertheless we, according to His promise, look for new heavens and a new earth in which righteousness dwells" (2 Peter 3:13).

Jesus Christ the "Sun of righteousness" (Malachi 4:2) will fill the presence of the new creation. Jesus Christ is God. God is light. The source of light will be God Himself. The glory of God will illuminate all of the new creation. God's radiance will illuminate all of creation for eternity future.

All created light, no matter how necessary here on earth, will be unnecessary in the new creation. It will be superseded by the perfect light shining, with its source the glory of God emanating from the person of Christ.

The nighttime to which we have grown accustomed will be gone forever. Nighttime, which represents evil, has no place there. Christians are children of the day, children of the light. In that day the Church will be like God Himself, of whom John wrote "in Him there is no darkness at all." The Church will shine with the full brilliance of God's light. One day this habitation we call earth will be left behind. God's people will be forever with Christ in the new creation. Christ Himself will be the light in the new creation.

We have seen that the sun is a picture of the Son. Just as the sun is the source of physical life, Jesus Christ is the source of spiritual life. In addition to the sun we also have a moon, and we know that the moon has no light of its own but merely reflects the sun's light. The moon is a picture of the true Church of Jesus Christ. The stars primarily represent the nation of Israel. God told the prophet Jeremiah that the stars would serve as a witness to the indestructibility of the Jewish race. "This says the Lord, Who gives the sun for a light by day, the ordinances of the moon and the stars for a light by night... 'If those ordinances depart from before Me, says the Lord, then the seed of Israel shall also cease from being a nation before Me forever'" (Jeremiah 31:35-36). Adolph Hitler is just one of the many who have tried to extinguish the Jewish race. God has ordained that it will not be so. "There is one glory of the sun, another glory of the moon, and another glory of the stars; for one star differs from another star in glory. So also, is the resurrection of the dead" (1 Corinthians 15:41-42).

There is a broader sense in which the stars represent the individual children of light. This is clearly seen in the Old Testament regarding Israel. Believers are individual lights and when they meet in a group they are like a chandelier.

Summary

Regarding the Light of the World, we find that there are three great lights. First, *we have the sun, which is truly the physical light of the world.* In Part One it became very clear that the sun is essential to our very existence.

Second, *Jesus Christ is the spiritual light of the world.* The greater light, our sun, is symbolic of that great spiritual light Jesus Christ. Just as the light from the sun provides physical life on our planet, so too the light from the Son provides spiritual life. Both forms of life, physical and spiritual, are initiated by the process of birth. As spiritual birth occurs in individuals, they become members of Christ's body, His Church. The Church is symbolized by the lesser light, the moon, having no light of its own but merely reflecting the Son's light.

Third, *the stars of our universe are a picture of God's people.*

Someday the true light of the cosmos, God Himself, will be the sole source of brilliance in the new heaven. There will be no need for the sun. Sonlight will be the sole source of light. For those who are members of the true Church, all will be light and truth. We shall be with Him forever and ever.

The concept of God light is composed of three elements within Scripture. First "God is light." Second, while on earth the Son of God was "the light of the world." He brought God light into focus. Finally, we are "children of light."

In Part One we looked at the Apostle John's statement "God is light" and the parallels between the nature of physical light and the attributes of spiritual light.

In Part Two the Light of the World was our focus.

In Part Three which will be presented in a future eBook we will examine parallels between the way physical objects react to physical light and how humans respond to spiritual light.

The next chapter will briefly review the vastness of Creation.

Sunlight / Sonlight

Sunlight reveals the beauty of creation.

Sonlight will return to take His followers to the beauty of the new creation.

THINK AND GROW

1. List three elements of "the light of the world" in Scripture.

2. List implications of having "no night or day" in the new creation (Zechariah 14:6, Revelation 22:5).

3. What role do you envision in the new creation for time, force, action, space, and matter?

28

The Vastness of Creation

A "light year" is the distance light travels in a year. At 286,282 miles per second, that comes to nearly six billion miles.

Big numbers are hard for most of us to comprehend.

It takes about seventeen minutes for 1,000 seconds to elapse. Twelve days contain about one million seconds. Thirty-two years contain about one billion seconds. For a trillion seconds to pass requires about 32,000 years (much longer than civilization has existed). A quadrillion seconds require 32,000,000 years (thirty-two million years). A quintillion seconds (10 with 18 zeros after it) require over thirty-two billion years.

Following are some statements from knowledgeable scientists and astronomers. Some of these statements are unverifiable. However, even if they are off by a factor of ten, they are beyond our comprehension. Keep in mind that as man's knowledge grows, these estimates are continually increasing!

Traveling at the speed of light, about 286,000 miles *per second*, it would take about 2,000 years to travel across our galaxy, the Milky Way. The Milky Way contains millions of stars (some estimates suggest over two billion stars). Our sun is one of those stars.

From our perspective the sun and its solar system seem huge, but if our Milky Way galaxy were the size of the North American continent, our sun and its entire solar system would be the size of a teacup.

Our sun is only an average-sized star. Within the Milky Way one star, the Pistol Star, produces one million times the energy of our sun. Yet in one second, our sun emits more energy than mankind has utilized throughout all of our history.

Our Milky Way galaxy is only a tiny part of the known universe. There are over 125 billion galaxies in the universe. Some experts believe the number to be more than a trillion galaxies.

Individual galaxies are believed to contain from 100 billion to a trillion stars.

The galaxy named UDFy-38135539 is estimated to be thirteen billion years old.

Some galaxies are more than thirteen billion light years from Earth.

In most cases, stars are separated by trillions of miles.

The total number of stars in the universe exceeds three trillion times 100 billion, or 300 sextillions (a three followed by twenty-three zeros). The scientifically revered Carl Sagan is well known for his comment that the total number of stars in the universe is greater than the total number of grains of sand on all the seashores of the earth.

There are quasars at the extreme edge of the known universe.

Some quasars are 1,000 times brighter than our Milky Way.

Some quasars emit more energy in one second than our sun does in ten million years.

The psalmist stated, "The heavens declare the glory of God" (Psalm 19:1).

The Master Craftsman is described in the eighth chapter of the Book of Proverbs, in its personification of wisdom. God is and the source of all wisdom.

Implications

In courtrooms of our time typically one credible witness is enough to establish a fact. Scripture states that in the mouth of two or three witnesses the truth can be established (i.e., Deuteronomy 17:6, 19:5; Matthew 18:16; 2 Corinthians 13:1; 1 Timothy 5:9). The reality of Jesus Christ on earth and His miracles is better established than any other historical figure of His time. Just one example—He was seen after His resurrection from the dead by over 500 eyewitnesses at one time (1 Corinthians 15:6).

Considering our vast universe, a choice seems clear. Option one is believing the conclusive evidence which supports the truth of Jesus Christ, the Son of God, who created everything (Hebrews 1:1-3).

"For by Him [Jesus Christ)] all things were created: things in heaven and on earth, visible and invisible, whether thrones or powers or rulers or authorities; all things were created by Him and for Him. He is before all things, and in Him all things hold together" (Colossians 1:16-17).

The second option is faith that accepts the concept that this vast universe "just happened" without a designer, from a beginning which lacked time, force, action, space, or matter.

Someone has remarked, "Since God created our magnificent earth in six days and He has already spent over 2,000 years creating His new creation, just try to imagine what it will be like!"

"I [Jesus Christ] go to prepare a place for you. And if I go and prepare a place for you, I will come again and receive you to Myself; that where I am, there you may be also" (John 14:2b-3).

Sunlight / Sonlight

Sunlight is the force which enables all life on earth—yet it is a tiny aspect of the total creation.

Sonlight reveals the truth yet what we know about the Son of God and His attributes is only a tiny part of the wonder and majesty of God.

THINK AND GROW

1. Looking deep inside all matter on earth we find a structure similar to the universe. Contemplate the psalmist's comment, "I am fearfully and wonderfully made" (Psalm 139:14).

2. Write an essay about this verse focusing at least partly upon the similarities between your body and outer space with its orbiting particles.

Epilog: Upward in a Flash

Einstein said, "The most beautiful thing we can experience is the mysterious. It is the source of all true art and all science." Sunlight is still not fully understood. Sonlight is not fully comprehended by even the children of light.

There are two stories about sunlight that have amused many. The first is about a class that had been taught about the tremendous speed of light that comes to us from the sun. The instructor was exclaiming the marvels of it all and then exclaimed, "Isn't it wonderful?" A voice from the back of the room replied, "It's not so great. After all, it's downhill all the way!"

The second is a comment that somebody once made. The substance of the comment was that the only thing that person knew about the speed of light was that he was glad it was becoming the time of year when light doesn't arrive so early in the morning!

These two anecdotes may make us smile, but we may be critical of anyone who seems so careless in regard to understanding the reality of light. It is tragic that so many are equally careless when it comes to understanding or investigating the reality of spiritual light. Unfortunately, some of us have not applied what understanding we do have of God in the same meticulous way that we have applied our understanding of physical light.

Part of the reason is that just as the physically dead person cannot perceive light, the spiritually dead person cannot perceive God. It requires physical birth to be sensitive to physical light, and it requires spiritual birth to be sensitive to spiritual light.

Those who perceive both physical and spiritual light realize that the two are intricately interwoven. For example, physical light, as we have seen, is related in a very basic way to all matter and energy. Concerning Jesus Christ, we read, "in Him all things hold together" (Colossians 1:17 niv), and "in Him we live and move and have our being" (Acts 17:28).

Those who have had a spiritual birth are reminded, "now *you are* light in the Lord. Live as children of light" (Ephesians 5:8), "that you may proclaim the praises of Him who called you out of darkness into His marvelous light" (1 Peter 2:9).

There is coming a time when Jesus Christ will return to earth. Listen to how Matthew describes the second coming of Christ: "For as the lightning comes from the east and flashes to the west, so also will the coming of the Son of Man be" (Matthew 24:27).

Light travels at a speed that would enable seven trips around the earth in one second. Light can circle this planet faster than you or I can wink. Jesus Christ has promised to return to earth for His church "in a flash" (1 Corinthians 15:52 niv). And "we know that when He is revealed, we shall be like Him" (1 John 3:2). Jesus Christ will be the visible light in all His glory in the new creation.

While suggesting some of the ways that our understanding of physical light allows us to more fully understand God, we have tried to understand what John meant when he was inspired by the Holy Spirit of God to write "God is light." It is the author's sincere prayer that each reader is able to say with John, "We have seen His glory" (John 1:14 niv), but always remembering "now we see in a mirror, dimly, but then face to face. Now I know in part, but then I shall know just as I also am known" (1 Corinthians 13:12).

THINK AND GROW

Are you walking in the light or just living in the light?

Please Consider This

If you liked this book, please leave a review online. Reviews help the authors you appreciate get recognized and help other readers choose what to read.

< **NOTE** >

There is a companion

follow-up book entitled

"GOD'S LIGHT: How To Respond"

(ISBN: 978-1393424994)

that compares

aspects of the behavior of sunlight

with the reactions of humans to Sonlight.

About the Author

Robert Lloyd Russell

Biography

Robert Lloyd Russell's books have won national and international literary awards including a World Book Award (one of just three awards across all genres). He is the editor of a book containing transcribed spoken messages of martyred missionary Jim Elliot. As a small boy Robert lived in the Elliot home at a time prior to Jim's departure for the mission field. The transcriptions were carefully made from old wire recordings, the forerunner of magnetic tape recordings. Jim was one of Robert's Sunday School teachers and Jim's father was one of his spiritual mentors.

Russell has a diverse secular background which spans many functions including engineering, manufacturing, sales, marketing, and staff positions. His technical career included the management of a wide variety of engineers, physicists, and scientists in the high-technology industry.

During the 1970s while he was Camera Engineering Manager for a Fortune 500 corporation, he became fascinated with the attributes of light and the parallels to the attributes of God. He would later write about these parallels in some of his books.

In the early 1970s a senior executive of a major corporation began seeking Robert's opinions and advice. This was the start of a part-time consulting business. Then, from 1990 until his retirement in 2005, Robert devoted his entire career to advising and coaching many executives in a variety of organizations. Based in Portland, Oregon, his consulting practice routinely provided coaching and counseling on a wide range of business issues including ethics, overall effectiveness and profitability, organizational cultural issues, and Total Quality concepts.

During the 1980s as an active Christian businessman concerned about ethics, Robert enrolled in seminary and earned a Master of Christian Leadership degree from Western Seminary. For many years he was a popular adult Sunday School and Bible Study teacher.

Robert refers to himself as a simple **A-B-C** kind of guy: Christian **A**uthor, Christian **B**logger, and Christian **C**onsultant and **C**oach. His blog entitled "Abundant Life Now[1]" has been read in nearly 200 countries and translated into more than 100 languages.

---

1. http://robertlloydrussell.blogspot.com/

Want Free Books?

As an author, I want to thank you for reading *SAMSON: Spirit-Filled to Self-Centered"* and I

regard the feedback of my readers very highly.

When considering buying a book many people weigh reviews carefully before deciding to purchase. If you enjoyed this book, would you consider assisting me by helping others make an informed decision? Leaving a review (even just a star rating without commentary) can help spread the message of the Gospel and increase others' faith through these books. It is also a great way to support this international ministry.

Robert Lloyd Russell's Newsletter[1]

Sign up for occasional updates from author Robert Lloyd Russell: https://www.subscribepage.com/rlr

He is committed to not bothering you with frequent newsletters. When he does send out occasional communications, it will contain one or more of the following:

- Advance information about current projects
- Related news
- Prayer requests
- Notification of **FREE eBooks** for a limited time
- Other items which may be of interest

---

1. *https://www.subscribepage.com/rlr*

(If you decide you no longer want to receive the newsletter, you may take advantage of the "unsubscribe" option at the bottom of each email.)

|||||

Robert Lloyd Russell's eBooks are available from your favorite online eBook retailer.

You may also want to visit the author's book website Books by Robert Lloyd Russell that lists his eBooks and printed books along with additional information, (booksrlr), or go to Books to Read[2] (https://books2read.com/ap/81Ym5B/Robert-Lloyd-Russell).

|||||

You are invited to connect with Robert Lloyd Russell through his daily internet blog *Abundant Life Now*[3] for inspiration and insight. (http://robertlloydrussell.blogspot.com/)

---

2. https://books2read.com/ap/81Ym5B/Robert-Lloyd-Russell

3. *http://RobertLloydRussell.blogspot.com/*

What To Read Next

"GOD'S NATURE: Sonlight—Sunlight" ISBN: 978-1393359371 ~ ASIN: B083L97PZV

An easy-to-read devotional style book which presents new and unforgettable insights. This landmark book identifies fascinating parallels between natural and spiritual light. Analogies teach profound truth in simple language.

"First there was Tozer with *The Knowledge of the Holy,* and then Packer gave us *Knowing God,* and now Russell has taken us further." —Dr. Earl D. Radmacher, General Editor, Nelson Study Bible/New King James Study Bible

Note: This eBook is an update of the first two sections of an earlier print book *GOD LIGHT: Sunlight Sonlight,* which **won six awards.**

Choose your favorite eBook retailer

https://books2read.com/GodsNature

"GOD'S CHILD: Like a Tree" ISBN: 978-1393518266 ~ ASIN: B0874CHLD7

Dr. Ronald B. Allen, a nationally recognized expert on the Psalms, described this book as "The definitive work on Psalm 1."

A timely book for those who long for faster, more consistent spiritual growth. In today's Christian communities many are complacent in their ultimate destination and they neglect the importance of the journey. In so doing, they miss out on many of the here and now benefits of their adoption into the family of God. The normal (not average) Christian is growing more like Jesus Christ as they continue their life on earth. If you long to be a disciple who pleases God, this book is for you. This book is extremely relevant to today's culture.

Choose your favorite eBook retailer

https://books2read.com/GodsChild

"GOD'S CHURCH: Christ's Pearl" ISBN: 978-1393268093 ~ ASIN: B07XFPMVQT ~ Print ISBN: 978-1393348597

Early in the book the author provides a straightforward look at the three most popular interpretations of the parable of the pearl of great price. Included is a clear Bible-based rejection of the common notion that the pearl represents salvation.

The major portion of the work provides parallels between the "one pearl of great price" and the Christian Church. Presented are seven unique aspects of a pearl which parallel the uniqueness of the Church. Finally, eight additional characteristics of a pearl and their parallels are presented.

Note: This eBook is an update of an earlier print book *ONE PRECIOUS PEARL: God's Design for His Church,* which **won five awards**.

Choose your favorite retailer (available as eBook or Print).

https://books2read.com/GodsChurch

"CHRIST'S DISCIPLE: How To Finish Strong" ISBN: 978-1393844402 ~ ASIN: B091XZF79B ~ Print ISBN: 979-8223262800

Written for those who long for faster, more consistent spiritual growth. Many in today's Christian communities are complacent about their ultimate destination and they neglect the importance of the journey. In so doing, they miss out on many of the here and now benefits of their adoption into the family of God. The normal (not average) Christian is growing more like Jesus Christ as they continue their life on earth. If you long to be a disciple who pleases God, this book is for you.

Choose your favorite retailer (available as eBook or Print).

https://books2read.com/ChristsDisciple

"GOD'S DESIRE: How To Please God" ISBN: 978-1393211785 ~ ASIN: B08H4F619W

This book develops two graphic models. The "Christian Life Model" is about victorious Christian living. Included in this section are the author's detailed acrostics for fellowship, obedience, power, prayer, witness, and the Word.

The "Christian Guidance Model" shows the interrelationship of the "Christian Life Model" and one's inner convictions, Godly counsel, and the Lordship of Jesus Christ.

Note: This eBook is an update of an earlier print book *"THY WILL BE DONE ON EARTH: Understanding God's Will for You."*

Choose your favorite eBook retailer

https://books2read.com/GodsDesire

"GOD'S LIGHT: How To Respond" ISBN: 978-1393424994

An easy-to-read devotional style book which identifies parallels between the reactions of physical objects to natural light and the reactions of humans to spiritual light. These analogies teach profound truth in simple language.

Written in short easily digestible segments, it is ideal reading for the person on the go. Readers gain a greater appreciation regarding Christians shining like lights.

Note: This eBook is an update of the third section of an earlier print book *GOD LIGHT: Sonlight Sunlight,* which won **six awards**.

Choose your favorite eBook retailer

https://books2read.com/GodsLight

"CHRIST'S BLOOD: 7+ Amazing Benefits" ISBN: 979-8201460877 ~ ASIN: B098W6LHVM

Understand the direct benefits to *you* from Christ's death and resurrection.

There are seven (plus one) directly stated benefits in Scripture.

Ponder ten additional benefits resulting from the Cross.

Choose your favorite eBook retailer

https://books2read.com/ChristsBlood

"TEMPTATION" 50+ Tips" ISBN: 979-8201564209 ~ ASIN: B0BCPN5YGW

Everyone is tempted (even Christ was)

50+ practical tips for personal victory over temptation!

Understand the battle and your spiritual weapons

Overcome the types of temptations you will face

Be confident and victorious in your Christian life

Choose your favorite eBook retailer

https://books2read.com/temptation-50tips

"PRIDE: Good and Bad" ISBN: 979-8201002053 ~ ASIN: B09SGSQLH9

Achieve a more consistent Christian life

As humans, we all have a common problem. Like rust to steel, pride is to our lives. Although there are examples of good pride in the Bible, most of the time pride is a negative part of our being.

Understanding the problem of pride is a vital part of gaining consistent spiritual victory as we live our daily lives.

Choose your favorite eBook retailer

https://books2read.com/Pride-Good-and-Bad

"SAMSON: Spirit-Controlled to Self-Centered" ISBN: 979-8215866122 ~ ASIN: B0BSZZSY8J ~ Print ISBN: 979-8223612964

The Biblical account of Samson's life includes ten significant victories interspersed among fifteen problematic events. How can we avoid a spiritually fickle life? What are the commonalities and contrasts between the lives of Samson and Christ? How did God evaluate Samson's life?

What practical lessons can we apply to our daily activities by looking at his life?

Choose your favorite retailer (available as eBook or Print).

https://www.booksrlr.com/ebooks/samson/

"PETER: Failure to Faith" ISBN: 979-8223422327 ~ ASIN: B0CBBC7DZC ~ Print ISBN: 979-8223315902

The Apostle Peter's Life in chronological order as he progresses from a fickle follower to a dynamic disciple.

This book can easily be a *fast read*. Due to small segments, it can also be used for *daily devotions* or in *short segments* by busy individuals. For scholars it can be the basis for a *lengthy personal study*. Small groups use it as a *spur to discussions*. Whatever your choice, enjoy as you read and reflect! Practical lessons for Daily Application.

Choose your favorite retailer (available as eBook or Print).

https://www.booksrlr.com/ebooks/peter-failure-to-faith/

"*JIM ELLIOT: Recorded Messages*" ISBN: 978-1393887959 ~ ASIN: B088FZ3XSC

Note: This eBook is an updated and significantly expanded version of an earlier print book "*JIM ELLIOT: A Christian Martyr Speaks to You.*"

Jim Elliot's spoken words transcribed for you – six practical messages with amazing depth and insight. These messages were given by this martyred Christian missionary before he left for the mission field in Ecuador. They were transcribed from a wire recorder, a forerunner of the magnetic tape recorder.

Christians of all maturity levels benefit from the understanding gained from Jim's discussions.

Choose your favorite eBook retailer

https://books2read.com/JimElliot

Print Book: ISBN: 978-0741475534 ~ *"GOD LIGHT: Sunlight Sonlight"* <u>won six awards</u> and is an easy-to-read devotional style book which presents new and unforgettable insights. This book identifies fascinating parallels between natural and spiritual light, and provides applications of natural and spiritual light. Analogies teach profound truth in simple language.

Available wherever quality print books are sold.

Note: There is an eBook update of the first two sections of this book entitled: *"GOD'S NATURE: Sonlight Sunlight."* The third section of this book is updated in the eBook entitled: *"GOD'S LIGHT: How To Respond."* Both are listed previously.

Print Book: ISBN: 978-0741462329 ~ *"ONE PRECIOUS PEARL: God's Design for His Church"* <u>won five awards.</u>

A straightforward look at the three most common interpretations of this parable.

The major portion of the book provides parallels between the "one pearl of great price" and the Christian Church.

Available wherever quality print books are sold.

Note: There is an eBook update of this book is entitled *"GOD'S CHURCH: Christ's Pearl."* It is listed previously.

Print Book: ISBN: 978-1606474310 ~ *"THY WILL BE DONE ON EARTH: Understanding God's Will for You"* is for those who are serious about living life in a way that pleases God.

Through the development of two graphic models the author provides insights regarding the interrelationship of fundamentals of the Christian faith.

Available wherever quality print books are sold.

Note: There is an eBook update of this book entitled *"GOD'S DESIRE: How To Please God."* It is listed previously.

Print Book: ISBN: 978-1615797646 ~ "*JIM ELLIOT: A Christian Martyr Speaks To You*" is directly relevant to all Christians.

Those with an interest in the history of missions or current missions will find the book riveting.

All Christians will appreciate Jim's straightforward, hard-hitting style of speaking.

Available wherever quality print books are sold.

Note: There is an eBook update of this book entitled "*JIM ELLIOT: Recorded Messages*." It has been enhanced and expanded with two additional messages and is listed previously.

Bibliography

Bragg, Sir William, O.M., K.B.E., D.SC., F.R.S.; *The Universe of Light*; New York, The Macmillan Company; 1933.

Calder, Nigel; *Einstein's Universe*; New York: The Viking Press; 1979.

Collis, John Stewart; *The World of Light*: New York: Horizon Press: 1960.

Cook, J. Gordan; *We Live By the Sun*; New York: The Dial Press; 1957.

Hurvich, Leo N.; *Color Vision*; Sunderland, MA: Sinauer Associates Inc.; 1981.

Jenkins, Francis A. & White, Harvey E.; *Fundamentals of Optics*; 4th Edition; McGraw-Hill; 1976.

Klein, H. Arthur; *Bioluminescence*; Philadelphia/New York: J. B. Lippincott Co.; 1965.

Minnaert, M.; *The Nature of Light and Color in the Open Air*; New York: Dover Publications, Inc.; 1954.

Morris, Richard; *Light*; Indianapolis/New York: The Bobbs-Merrill Co., Inc.; 1979.

Ruchlis, Hy.; *The Wonder of Light: A Picture Story of How and Why We See*; New York: Harper & Brothers; 1960.

Sagan, Carl; *Cosmos*; New York: Random House; 1980.

Sanders, J. H.; *Velocity of Light*; New York: Pergamon Press; 1965.

Sheard, Charles, Ph.D., Sc.D.; *Life-Giving Light*; New York: The Century Co.; 1933.

Smith, Warren J.; *Modern Optical Engineering: The Design of Optical Systems*; McGraw-Hill; 1966.

Smithsonian Exposition Books; *Fire of Life*; New York: W. W. Norton & Co.; 1981.

[1] Dr. Robert John Russell (no relation to the author), Founder and Director, The Center for Theology and the Natural Sciences.

[2] Morris, Richard, *Light* (Indianapolis / New York: The Bobbs-Merrill Co., Inc., 1979), page 98.

[3] Ibid.

[4] Calder, Nigel, *Einstein's Universe* (New York: The Viking Press, 1979), page 2.

[5] Ibid, page 99.

[6] Sheard, Charles, Ph.D., Sc.D., *Life-Giving Light* (New York: The Century Co., 1933), page 126.

[7] Smithsonian Exposition Books, *Fire of Life* (New York: W. W. Norton & Co., 1981), page 14.

[8] Collis, John Stewart, *The World of Light* (New York: Horizon Press, 1960), page 26.

[9] Cook, J. Gordan, *We Live By The Sun* (New York: The Dial Press, 1957).

[10] Sagan, Carl, *Cosmos* (New York: Random House, 1980), page 212.

[11] Collis, John Stewart, *The World of Light* (New York: Horizon Press, 1960), page 16.

[12] Three reactions; absorption, refraction, and reflection. Three types of light sources; a ray of light, a pencil of light, and a beam of light. Three parameters in equations of geometric optics; time, area, and the solid angle.

[13] Smithsonian Exposition Books, *Fire of Life* (New York: W.W. Norton & Co., 1981), page 17.

[14] Bartlett, John, *Familiar Quotations*, edited by Emily Morison Beck, 14th Edition (Boston: Little, Brown & Co., 1968), page 950.

[15] Ibid, page 95.

[16] Pauling, Linus, *College Chemistry: An Introductory Textbook of General Chemistry* 2nd Edition (San Francisco: F.W.H. Freeman and Co., 1957), page 60.

Don't miss out!

Visit the website below and you can sign up to receive emails whenever Robert Lloyd Russell publishes a new book. There's no charge and no obligation.

https://books2read.com/r/B-A-QQUI-YELCB

BOOKS2READ

Connecting independent readers to independent writers.

Also by Robert Lloyd Russell

Bible Character Series
Samson: Spirit-Controlled to Self-Centered
Peter: Failure to Faith

Christian Concepts Series
God's Church: Christ's Pearl
God's Nature: Sonlight Sunlight
God's Child: Like a Tree

Christian Growth Series
God's Desire: How To Please God
God's Light: How To Respond
Christ's Disciple: How To Finish Strong

Christian Theology Series
Christ's Blood: 7+ Amazing Benefits
Pride: Good and Bad
Temptation: 50+ Tips

Missions
Jim Elliot: Recorded Messages

Watch for more at www.booksrlr.com.